More Sweaters

More Sweaters
A Riot of Color, Pattern, and Form

Lise Kolstad & Tone Takle

INTERWEAVE PRESS

This book was developed in cooperation with J.W. Cappelens Forlag and
Rauma Uldvarefabrikk

English translation: Arnhild Hillesland
Photography: Guri Dahl except as follows: Photos on pages 55, 57, 87, 88, 84, 103, 106, 112, 114, 115, 122, and 125 by Joe Coca
Illustrations: Lise Kolstad
Technical Editor: Dorothy Ratigan
Cover Design: Susan Wasinger/Signorella Graphic Arts
Production: Marc McCoy Owens

printed in Hong Kong by Sing Cheong

Interweave Press, Inc.
201 East Fourth Street
Loveland, Colorado 80537
USA

Library of Congress Cataloging-in-Publication Data
Kolstad, Lise.
[Strikk hva du vil. English]
More sweaters : a riot of color, pattern and form / Lise Kolstad and Tone Takle.
p. cm.
ISBN 0-934026-99-8 : $19.95
1. Knitting—Patterns. 2. Sweaters. I. Title
TT825.K6813 1994
746.43'20432—dc20 94-27968
CIP

First Printing:IWP—10M:994:CC

Contents

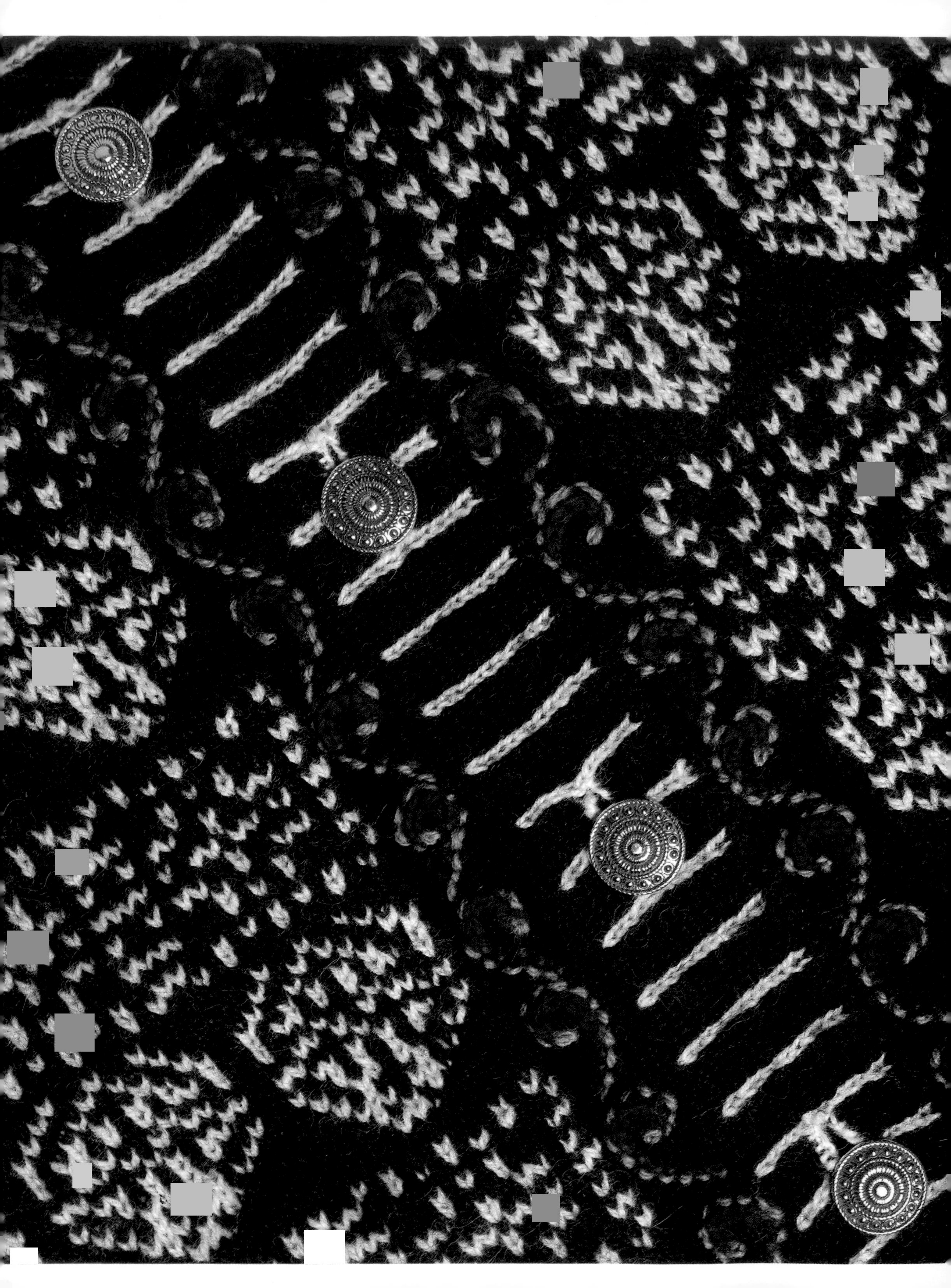

INTRODUCTION

For those of us who knit, the requirements of use and function are high. Much of the joy of knitting is in making something beautiful and, at the same time, functional. Yet, often when we try new ideas, they end up as disasters. Should this stop us from learning something new? We think not. This book is for all knitters who wish to renew themselves. We will pass on some of our own experiences regarding needles and yarn, but concentrate on your creating your own designs. Although some of your most fantastic ideas might very well end up as disasters, we feel that it is through trial and error that we learn new skills.

There are several risks involved with knitting a garment. Knitting takes time, and the yarn costs can run high if you do a lot of knitting. We recommend that all passionate knitters buy a ball of each color of their favorite yarn and make swatches in order to learn about colors and designs without being concerned about the final product. By spending time experimenting, you will gain experience that gradually will make you a more competent and creative knitter.

It might seem overwhelming to create your own garment pattern. Eight to ten years ago, when we could not seem to find enough patterns to knit, we collected everything from embroidery designs to very old knitting patterns. We did a lot of experimenting with the shapes of the garments and combinations of colors before we tried to create our own patterns.

You may look upon design as something close to magical—even mystical—and something you do not do on your own because it is too complex. Actually, many designs are quite simple. Icelandic sweaters, for example, are decorated with simple variations of dots, and Fana sweaters (from Fana, near Bergen, Norway) have starred and striped borders. Simplicity can often be so beautiful that we do not realize how easy the designing can be.

You can tap into ornamental design influences from European cathedrals or look at the borders of yellowed needlework books. The methods described in this book focus on creating an original piece of knitted work from beginning to end.

Our goal has not been to produce an encyclopedia of knitting or to detail a particular knitting technique or style, such as lace knitting or gansey knit. Instead, we've described a basic work method that you can build on. We have given you some food for thought concerning colors and materials and some helpful tips for creating your own designs. The rest is up to you.

In the beginning of the book, we describe work methods and supplies. Then, we look at simple designs such as dots and stripes and how you can use them in varied ways. After that, we will study more complex designs such as stars and flowers. Finally, we'll describe some basic techniques of knitting for beginners and guide you through creating your own knitting patterns from scratch.

Our experiences with the use of color and experiments with materials have not been explored in great detail in this book. We would rather not hinder you in any way with theories on what is beautiful and what is not and with thoughts on what colors go together which ones do not. Use of color and material is a personal matter. We have been inspired while experimenting with "strange" types of yarn and by looking at art, clothes, and natural materials. Whenever we discuss the use of color in this book, it is to give you some idea of what is at your disposal.

The use of material is a huge and exciting world in itself. The most commonly used and well-known materials are cotton and wool. By choosing a theme like matt/shiny, soft/hard or thick/thin, you will probably discover many new materials and means of expression. When you have learned to create designs and write your own patterns, the courage to experiment with colors and materials will naturally come to you. Throughout this book you will find pictures of garments showing what we have learned about colors, shapes, materials, and designs. We hope these will be of some inspiration to you as you work with your own designs. We have also included complete patterns on all the garments shown in the book. This might seem a bit contrary to our purpose of encouraging you to create your own designs, but we do not want knitters who still like to use patterns to feel cheated by looking at pictures of garments without being able to knit them exactly the way they look.

The sweaters we have created are large. On page 136 is a table with all the measurements for width and length of both the sleeve and the body for each pattern. It is a good idea to take measurements of the person who is to wear the garment before you decide on a size in order to avoid some unpleasant surprises when the garment is done. We also suggest that you read through the whole pattern before you start knitting. In the section on knitting techniques, some methods are described in more detail. For example, if the pattern calls for two needle sizes, this usually means that you need double-pointed needles in the smallest size and both sizes of 16" and 24" circular needles. It is important that you knit to the given gauge to ensure proper fit.

It is up to you how you use this book. You can flip through it, look at the pictures, and knit using our patterns. You can get ideas from different designs and create your own garments, or you can create something entirely new. One way is not better or worse than another. But if you feel that this book has given you more knitting pleasure, we have achieved our goal. The most important thing is for you to take yourself seriously enough to invest in both experiments and experiences that can make you a knitter "in motion".

We would like to thank Kari Skodvin of Cappelen Fakta, and photographer Guri Dahl for their cooperation, Hotel Alexandra in Loen, Norway for their kindness and assistance during photography sessions, and Rauma Uldvarefabrikk for making it possible for us to do this book.

Tone and Lise

ABOUT SUPPLY AND METHOD

To make designs, you need graph paper. The squares should approximate a knitted stitch, or it will be difficult to get an accurate idea as to how the design will look once it is knitted.

To draw patterns, you need markers. If you make a mistake drawing, you should glue some graph paper over the mistake and try again instead of using correction fluid. The former method produces better copies.

It is helpful if you have access to a copy machine. You can, of course, do fine without the copier, especially on simple designs. But if you want to make designs that span several stitches, a copy machine is extremely valuable. If you have to do everything by hand, it will take a long time to draw enough repeats to give you an idea of the complete design.

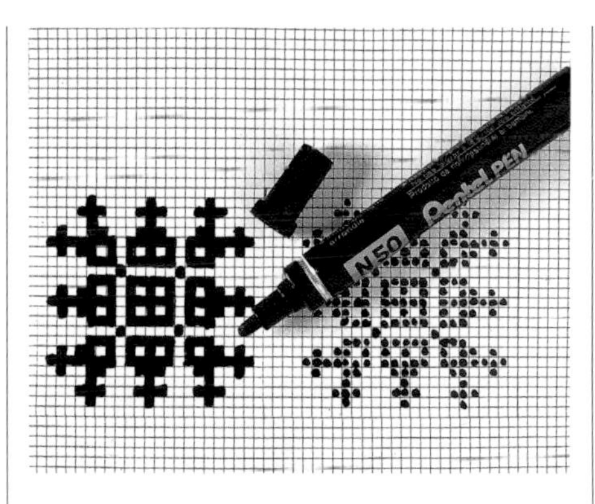

We show only a few repeats of each design in this book because space is limited. When we design for ourselves, we always use large sheets of paper, such as 17 inches × 11 inches. This makes it easier to see how the design will look when it is knitted. You can cut out the bad repeats without spending the time knitting them, only to find out how bad they look. When you make copies of designs, you can also try out the same detail in different variations easily. You often do not see the possibilities of a pattern until you have moved different pieces around on graph paper for a while.

There are several ways of putting designs on paper. You can make a dot in the middle of each square, or you can fill the whole square. Decide which method is faster or easier for you to read. In this book, the filled squares represent a contrast color, and the open squares represent the main color.

Instead of building up a design by filling in the individual squares, you can start by drawing lines for the whole design on the graph paper with a pencil and then fill in the squares covering the lines you drew. If you make letters, numbers, or motifs that are somewhat rigid, this is a good method to use. Other designs should first be drawn freehand, and then transferred onto graph paper. This method might be used to create a floral and leaf design with flowing lines, a design that would not be easy to imagine on graph paper.

It is a good idea to keep your patterns in a folder with plastic pockets. Then you will have them all in one place. Designs you do not think much of now might become interesting later on, so you should keep everything you design.

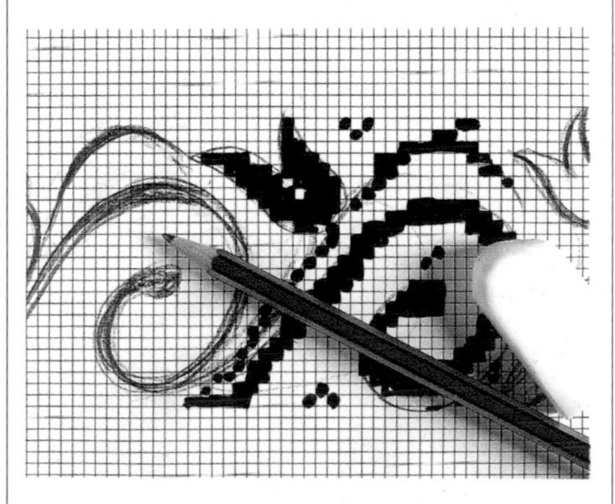

Swatches

The best way to make swatches is to use double-point needles. Knitting in the round goes faster than knitting of back and forth. Cast on forty to fifty stitches, depending on how large your design is. Cut the swatch after you are done and steam it. Using a sewing machine, zigzag the edges to keep them from unraveling.

We usually put labels on prospective swatches, and write down what we are pleased with or any changes we would like to make in color and/or design. Or, we simply write down what we tried to achieve in order to remember it later. Hold on to all your swatches, whether you like them or not, as they might become useful later.

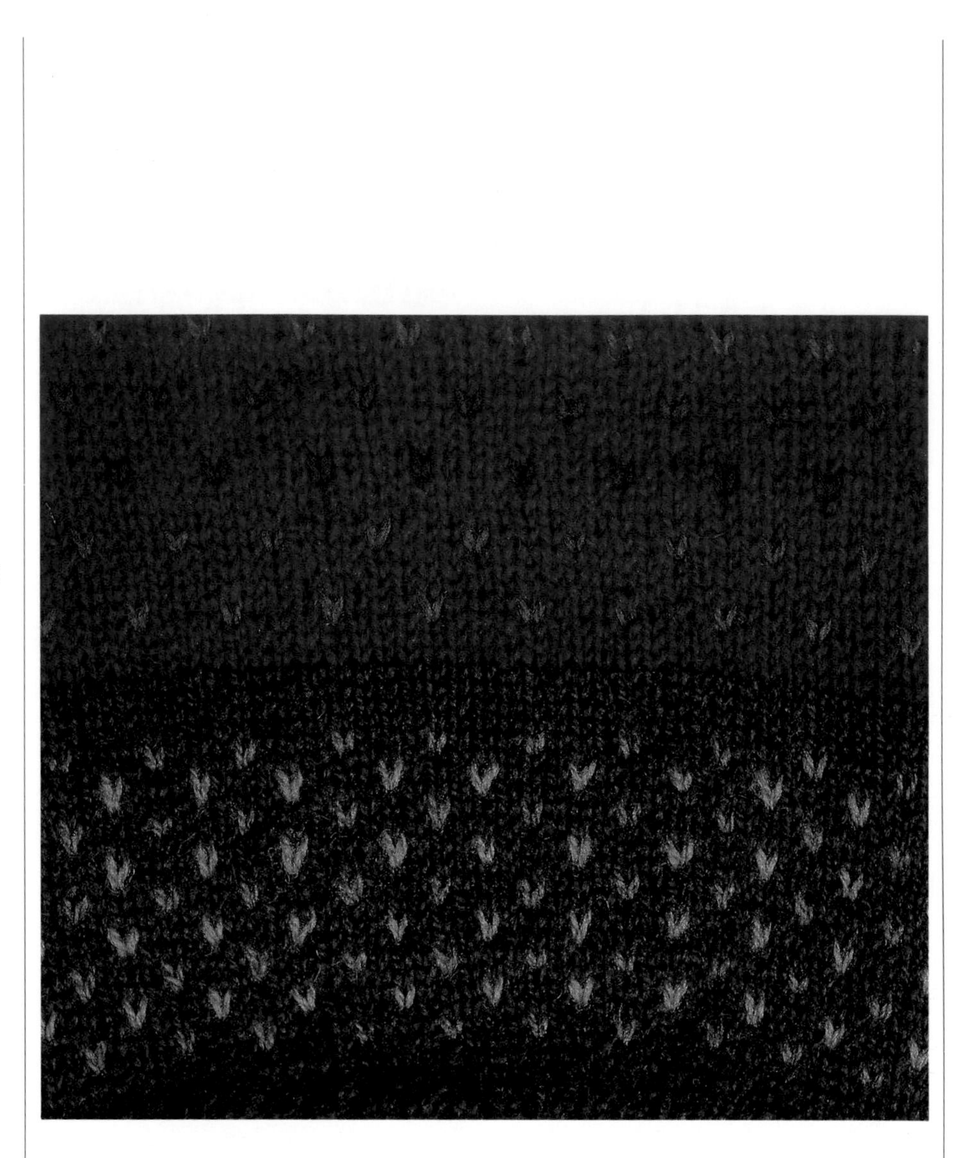

PART 1
PLAIN DESIGNS

DOTS

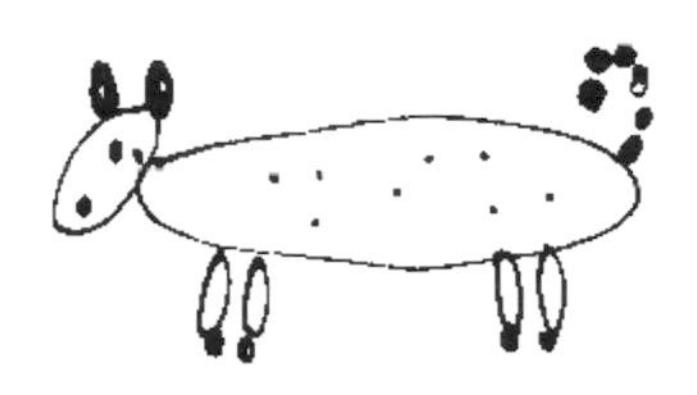

We will begin with the easiest of all designs: dots. This is a good starting point if you are new to designing your own borders.

Simple designs only have a repeat of a few stitches. It is easy to understand how they are built up, and it does not take long to learn them by heart when knitting.

Simple is not the same as boring. Small designs can be beautiful and provide many possibilities for variations of colors and materials. Also, small designs often need to be used with large designs to keep them from becoming too overwhelming.

Dots, or lice as they are called among knitters, are among the easiest of all designs. Still, they offer enormous possibilities for different combinations. You can have a short or long distance between the lice and few or many rounds between each row of lice. The lice can be placed in rows right on top of one another or slanted, or they can be in groups of twos. There are more possibilities than one might think.

Try it yourself. With a pencil, mark off ten to twelve squares on graph paper and see how many variations of dots you can think of. Make swatches of some of the designs. They are so easy to do that you can experiment with colors and end up with many exciting ideas.

A. The lice are placed evenly above one another.

B. The lice are moved over one square for each row of lice, creating a design with diagonal lines.

C. The lice are spread evenly across the surface, but are not placed evenly above one another.

D. The lice are closer together, and there are more stitches between them in height than in width.

E. There are lice in every round, but they are not placed evenly above one other. This design makes a dense, almost varigated surface.

F. The lice are still close together, but are evenly spread out to all sides.

G. The lice are placed in pairs, but with more space around them. This design is often used in Icelandic sweaters.

H. The lice are also in pairs, but closer together. This design has a different effect than G.

I. The dots are made with four stitches (and can no longer be called lice). This design has a more powerful effect than when only single stitches are knitted in a contrast color.

J. The lice have plenty of room in width, but not in height. To the eye, they appear as stripes.

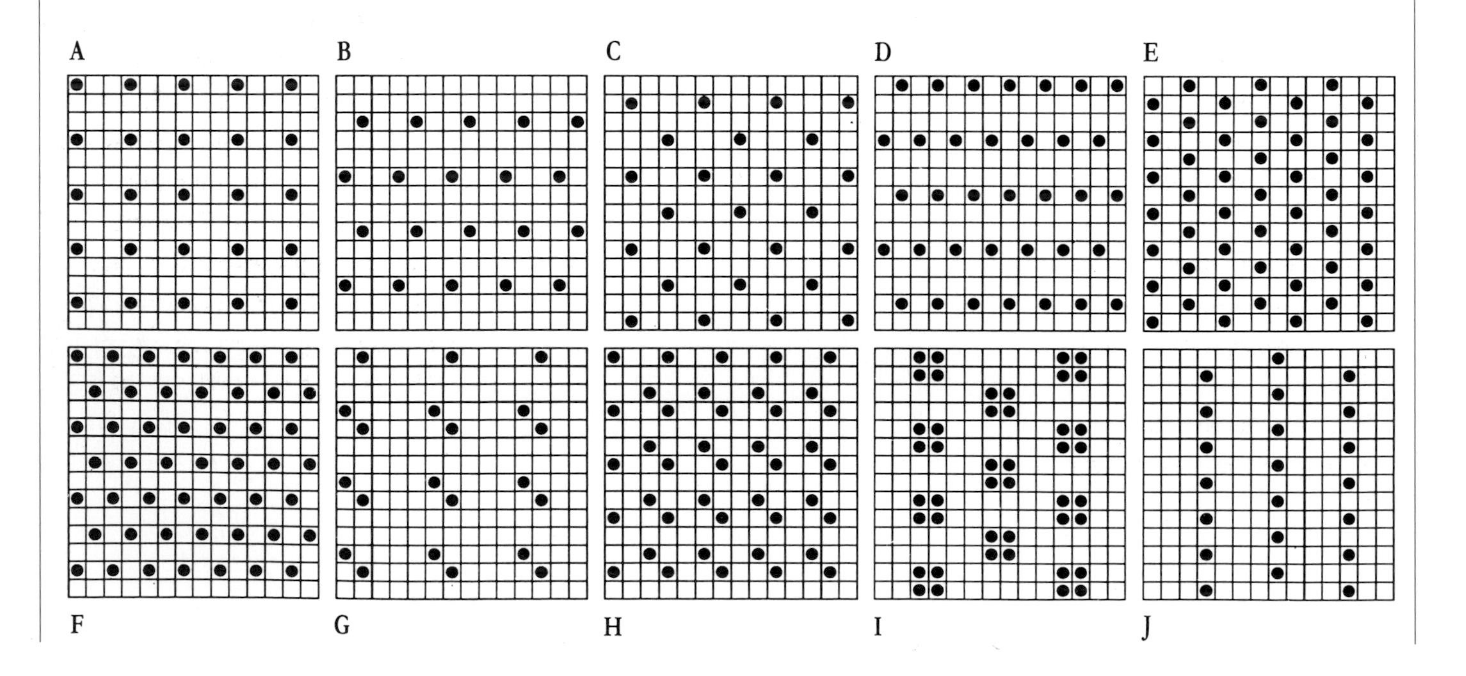

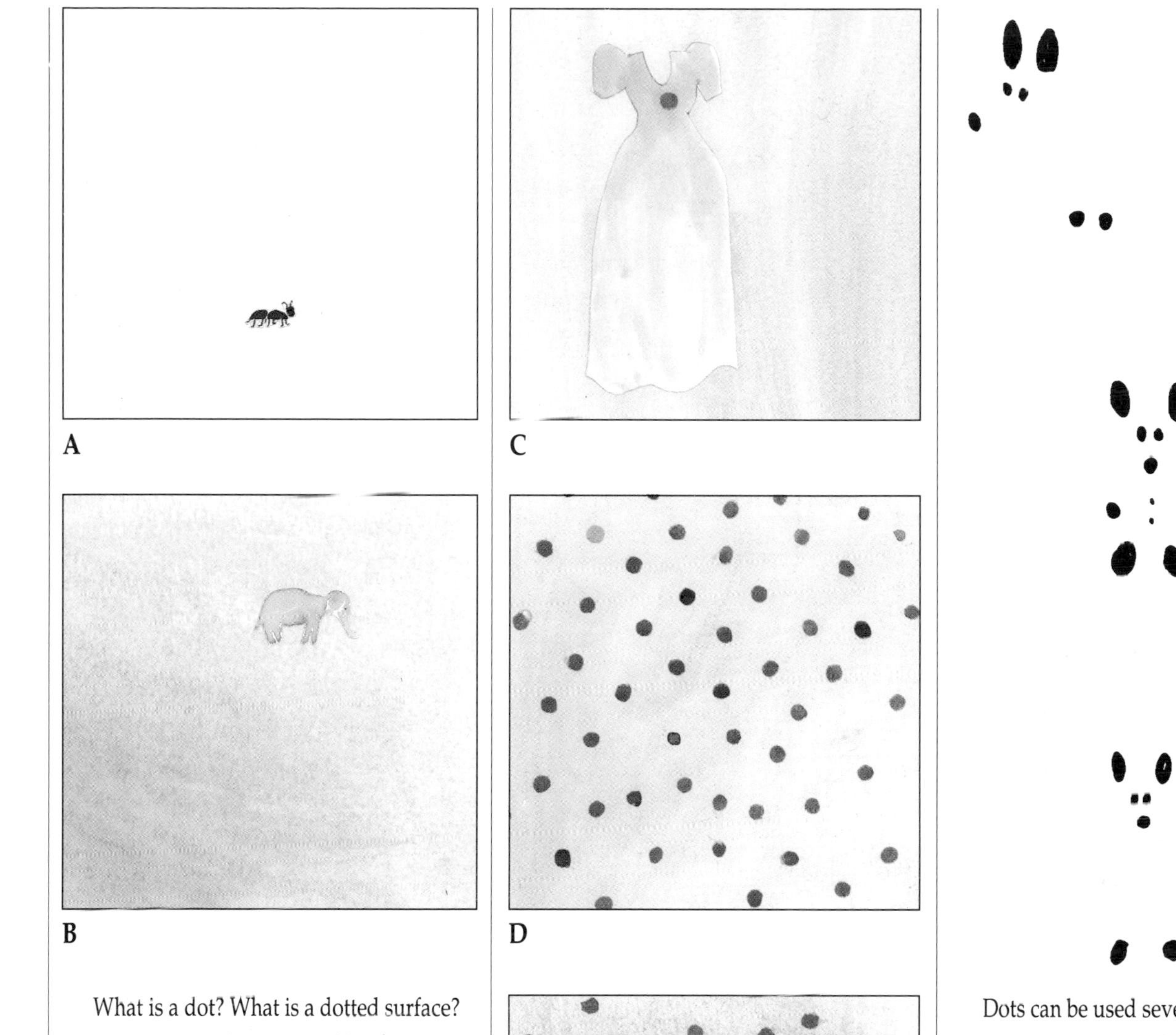

What is a dot? What is a dotted surface?

A. An ant can be perceived by the eye as a dot if it is far away.

B. The same is true for an elephant.

C. A dress with one dot is not a dotted dress. A dotted design has more than one dot. It consists of a small shape repeated several times on a surface. Or it can be several small shapes repeated over and over again.

D. This is a dotted surface.

E. Here are dots on a dotted surface.

E

Dots can be used several ways in a knitted garment. They can be the main pattern, as on an Icelandic sweater, or they can be a plain or calmer design, to which you can add larger designs, as on the sweaters from Setesdal, Norway. They can also be the background for larger designs. By knitting large roses, stars, letters, reindeer, and other motifs with dots you can prevent having very long strands at the back of your work.

STRIPES

Stripes can be placed horizontally and vertically. They can all be the same width, vary in width, or be placed harmoniously in groups. Stripes can form a fine background for other and bigger designs, as in Model 9. Vertical stripes can be used as borders on sleeves and collars, they can serve as additional designs, or they can be used on a sleeve when it is difficult to increase stitches in the main design. For example, in Model 2, the sleeve and the body have striped gussets. The same technique can be used on the sides of a sweater where the body gradually increases.

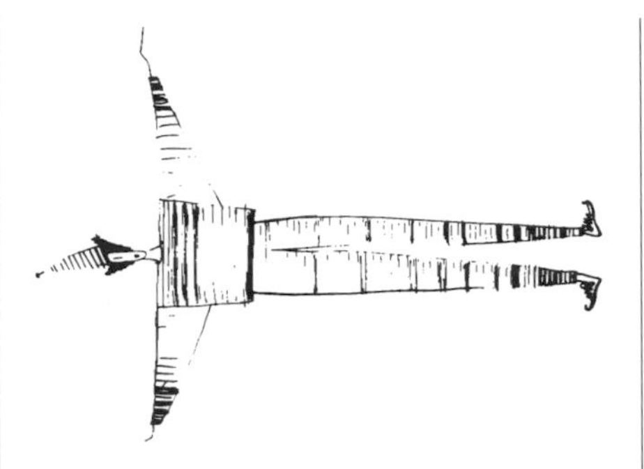

A. Narrow stripes.

B. Slightly wider stripes. These stripes are suitable as background for a bigger design as well as an alternative to regular ribbing for sleeves, collars, et cetera.

C. Wide stripes placed closer together.

D. Narrow stripes placed farther apart.

E. and F. Wide and narrow stripes placed together in repetitive sequences.

A

B

C

D

E

F

If you do not want to think too much about design, then let the colors be the most important element in your garment. Horizontal stripes can be a good way to use color. A design with very narrow stripes doesn't look busy because the colors seem to blend into one. Knitting narrow stripes is also a nice way to use up your leftover yarn. Make a striped sweater or practice stripes by knitting shocking tights. There are several patterns for tights in this book.

Stripes have rhythm. Bolsters, a type of woven wool coverlet, often have an exciting array of stripes. The same goes for many rag rugs. It may sound strange, but try to "speak" the stripes you make. Narrow stripes are a short sound. Wide stripes are a long sound. By speaking the sounds in this way, you will experience the excitement of the stripes. You do not have to "recite stripes" for an audience, but at least think about stripes as rhythm. Spend some time looking at them, and ask others their opinion. Do not give up before you find a composition that you like.

Maybe you will say stripes are just stripes, and leaf through the book for more difficult topics. Don't do that! Stripes are about composition, and knowledge of composition will help you make more complex designs. You'll also need to understand dimensions when you arrange borders on a garment. Just as a piece of music needs a beat and a movie should engage you, a sweater needs a rhythm. In addition to being a garment, a sweater is a composition, even if it is not a "Top 40" hit.

Why does "everyone" wear the Per Spook sweater, the Setesdalkofte, or the Fana sweater? It is because these sweaters have "just the right" composition.

Stripes are a good gateway through which to learn about composition. If you make a sweater with nicely blended borders, the eye's attention is not unnecessarily drawn to them. However, without harmony, people will notice that something is not quite right. If you make a striped sweater that lacks an exciting arrangement between narrow and wide stripes, it will be obvious to all. Therefore, it is necessary to create a well-designed striped pattern. And if you succeed in doing that, your borders should harmonize as well. Instead of drawing a striped pattern, you can make a "sketch" using pieces of yarn wound around a piece of cardboard. Then you do not spend a lot of time trying out ideas before you start drawing and knitting. It is easier to achieve a successful design if the stripes form a steady rhythm. Excitement develops when contrasts interact, either as light and dark colors or as narrow and wide stripes.

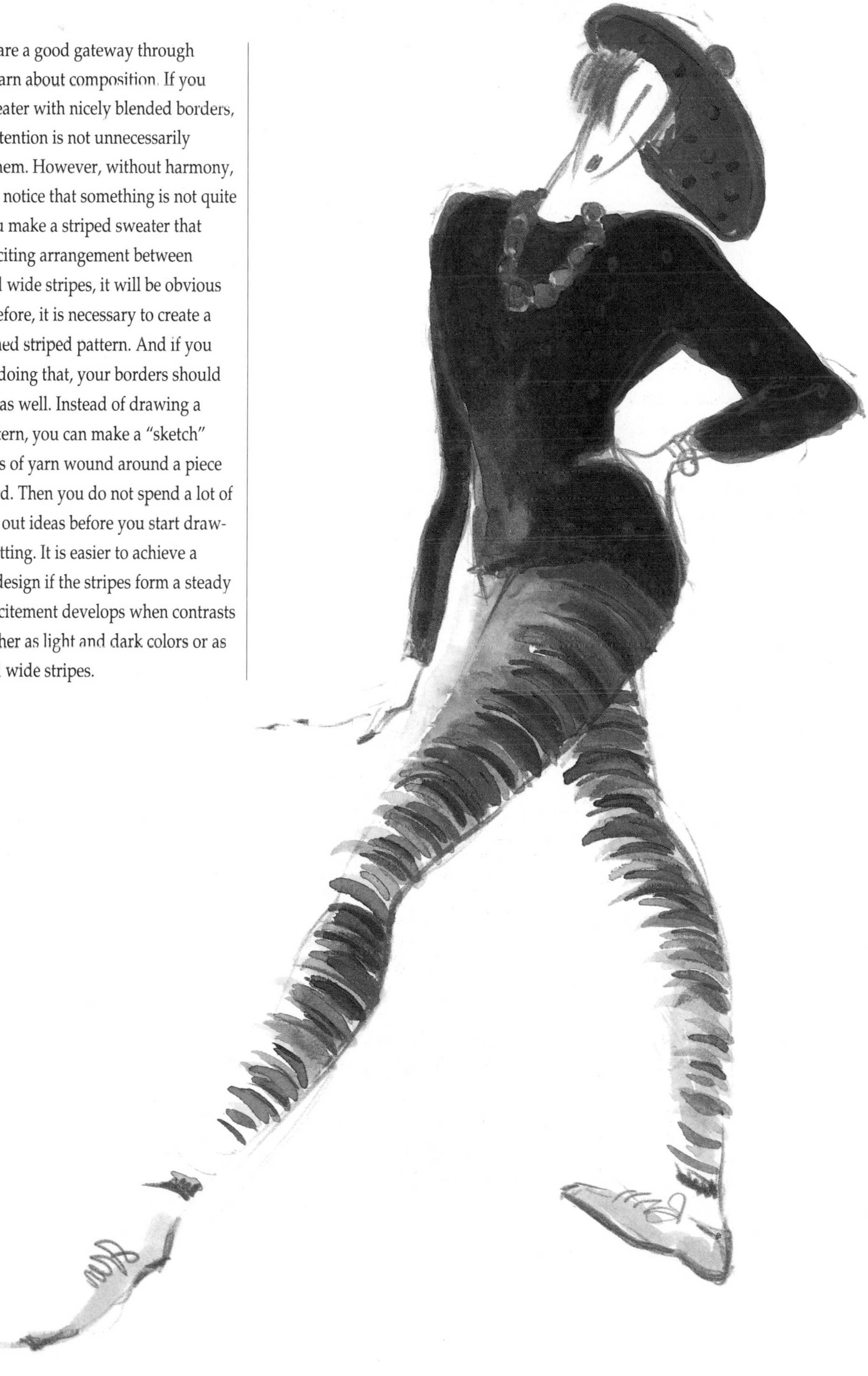

a b c d e f g

a. and b. See how a wide blue stripe seems more dominating than a wide orange stripe.

c. and d. Here, the wide stripes are made wider, while the narrow ones remain the same.

e. and f. The wide stripes are made even wider. But if they get too wide compared to the narrow stripes, the design will loose its character.

g. This design consists of three colors instead of two. Blue is the darkest color, which is why we see it as the "heaviest", or the main color. Of the two orange shades, the darkest is the "heaviest". Let us return to the language of music. This design has rhythm—the blue stripes are heavily emphasized, the dark orange is somewhat lighter, and the light orange is the least emphasized.

h. In the previous example, the two orange stripes have the same width. Here, the lightest stripes are wider, which gives them more power. Do you find the two orange stripes being equally "heavy"? There is an interesting tension between light and heavy and light and dark in this striped composition.

i. Once again, the orange stripes have the same width, but now the blue stripes seem too narrow with the abundance of orange. The whole composition is almost too loud.

j. and k. The two lightest colors dominate, while the blue helps to tighten the whole composition. It is only the width of the orange stripes that vary in j and k, but notice how different they are. Which sample do you think works best?

l. The orange stripes are, once again, narrow, and they seem as if they are put on top of the blue background. The rhythm of the colors are like a waltz: heavy-light-light.

Even if the same "repeat" of stripes is not repeated over the whole surface, it is a good idea to decide on certain sizes for the stripes. For example, you could have 1, 3, and 7 rounds of each color. This would give the surface a look of completion, even if the different sizes are not knitted in a certain order.

DIAGONAL-STRIPED DESIGNS

When you design for knitting, you can not be totally free with your drawing. The difference in making a knit design and an ordinary drawing is like building with wooden blocks as compared to working with clay. Soft and rounded forms must be replaced by squares where one square on the graph paper is equivalent to one stitch in your knitting. The limitations of designing on graph paper might seem to be a hinderance at first, but it will soon become a welcome challenge.

A. A wide stripe alternated with a narrow stripe has more effect than stripes that are exactly the same. Here, light and heavy slanted stripes alternate.

B. Light slanted stripes, single and in pairs, create a rhythm.

C. The stripes change direction as they go along.

D. The stripes are moved one stitch to the side every fourth round. In this way, the stripes will not slant as much as when the stitches are moved in every round.

E. The stripes are moved one stitch to the side alternating every second and third round.

F. When the stripes are moved as irregularly as here, they create waves.

G. Diagonal lines changing directions create a zigzag design. Here, the stripes are broken up, but they still look like zigzag stripes.

H. A combination of straight and zigzag stripes.

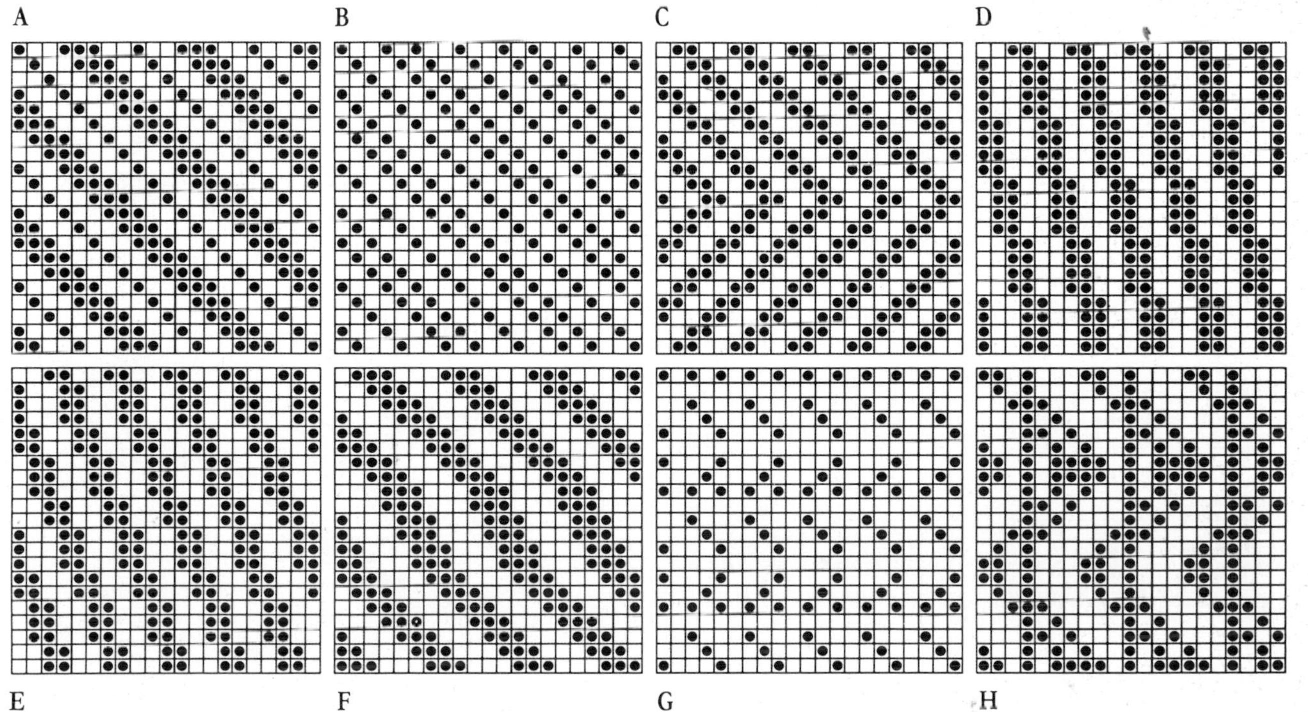

A. In this diagonal design, the slanted stripes turn in the middle of each repeat. Each repeat is finished off with horizontal stripes.

B. Here, the diagonal borders alternate between the main color and the contrast color as to which is dominant. In addition, the tip of the diagonal borders change direction. Model 1 shows how a striped design can be used in different ways in a sweater. In Border 1, a diagonal border from B is combined with a completely different border. The result is quite refreshing. Border 2 gives a new variation of the same theme. Here, the zigzag is constantly changing direction, so the design alternates between squares and Xs.

C. and D. You can break up a zigzag border by adding space at the intersection between the two slanted stripes. By doing this, you will create a curved line and a sort of marbled look. One of the diagonal stripes here is heavier than the other. The distance between the curved lines are greater in D than in C, but it can also be somewhere in between, as in Model 16, Border 1.

C

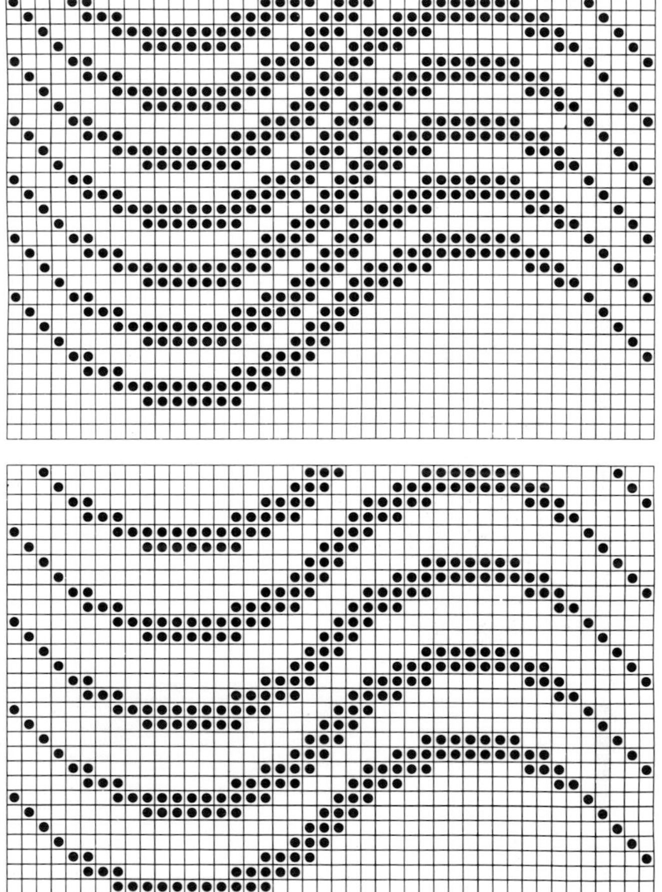

D

A

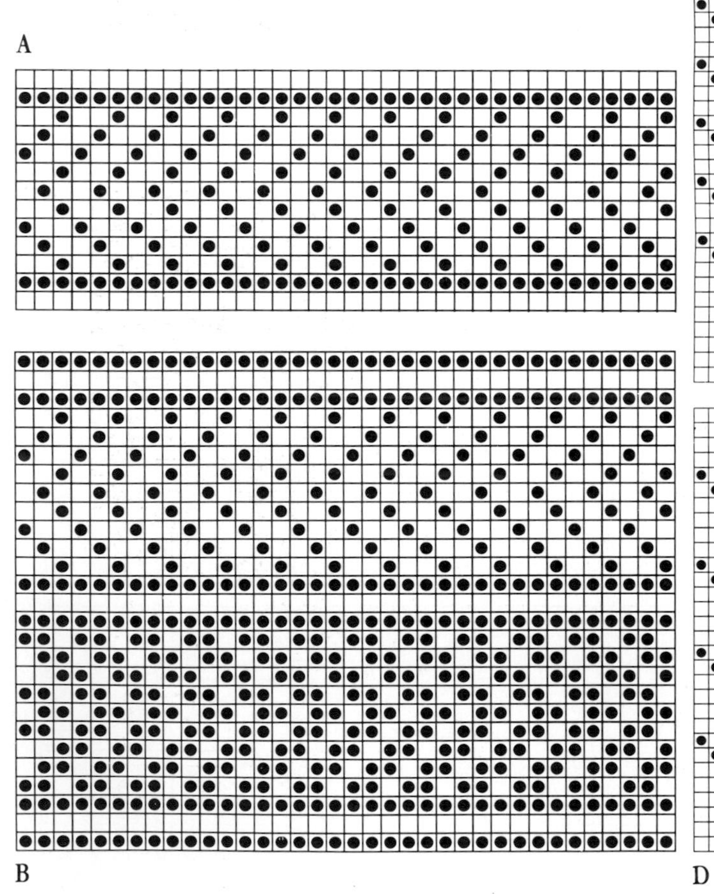

B

E. and F. Curved diagonal stripes can be put together to create a trellis design. Notice that alternating between thick and thin lines makes the design softer and more alive, compared to lines that have the same thickness throughout the design.

Try this yourself by dividing your graph paper into even squares and drawing all the slanted lines you can think of. Make eight to ten copies of your sheet, cut out the small squares, and move them around on a separate piece of graph paper. See how many different designs you can make with your squares. Think of stripes, zigzag lines, squares, trellises, et cetera. Make designs that build on top of each other in height and borders that lay next to each other in width, or make some designs that change along the way. Pick the design you like best and make swatches using many variations of color, making each one as different from the other as possible. Colors have a great impact on how the design will look.

E

F

MODEL 1

SWEATER WITH BIRD BORDERS

Diagonal stripes, flowers, birds, and vertical stripes form the design on this sweater. The design on the body is dominant and the sleeve design is relatively calm. On the body, diagonal borders are placed at the edge to frame the bird borders. This makes the vertical lines eye catchers. This sweater design was not difficult to draw or to knit, but the planning of this sweater required some extra forethought. It is simpler to make designs using horizontal stripes in a more traditional way.

YARN: Rauma Finullgarn. The sweater shown is knit in the colors listed below.

CHARTS: pages 26–27

SIZES: S (M, L, XL, XXL)

COLORS: #401 White 350 (400, 450, 500, 550)g; #414 Charcoal 300 (350, 400, 450, 500)g

GAUGE: 27 stitches and 32 rounds = 4 × 4 inches

NEEDLE SUGGESTION: Circular and double-point knitting needles size 2.5mm and 3mm, or size necessary to obtain gauge. It is very important to knit to gauge otherwise the garment will be too big or too small.

BODY: Using smaller circular needle and Charcoal, cast on 234 (260, 286, 312, 338) stitches. Knit in the round for 1¼ inches. Purl 1 round, and knit 3 rounds. Join White. Work Border 1 for 4 inches. Change to larger needle. With Charcoal, knit 3 rounds increasing or decreasing to 244 (260, 276, 308, 340) stitches evenly spaced on the second round. The width of Panel 3 on Border 1 varies according to the size of the sweater and consists of 29 (37, 45, 61, 77) stitches. Beginning at left side seam, *knit 1 stitch in White ("seam stitch"), work Border 2 as follows: Panel 1, 2, 3, 4, and 1. Rep from*. In addition to Border 2, worked on the front and on the back, the sweater has stripes on each side. The stripes consist of alternating 1 stitch of each color. These stitches originate by increasing 1 stitch on each side of the White seam stitches. Continue to work Border 2 increasing 1 stitch in stripe pattern on each side of the seam stitches every 6th round 10 times until you have 284 (300, 316, 348, 380) stitches total. Work until the sweater measures 10¾ (13½, 12¾, 11, 13¾) inches. Bind off 21 stitches centered at each underarm: 242 (258, 274, 306, 338) stitches. On the next round, cast on 2 stitches over the bound-off stitches. Purl these 2 stitches on every row using both strands of yarn. They are to be machine stitched and cut open for sleeve openings. Continue working in the round until you have finished the 4th (5th, 5th, 5th, 6th) loop of the acanthus vine (Panels 2 & 4). Begin Border 3 at size marker. Work 13 (13, 7, 7, 7) rounds total. Bind off the center front 39 (39, 39, 41, 41) stitches for the neck. Work back and forth through the 28th round of Border 3. Work the same neck shaping on the back as you did for the front. Finish Border 3. Put the stitches on a holder.

SLEEVES: Using smaller double-point needles and Charcoal, cast on 52 stitches. Knit in the round. Work the hem and Border 1 as you did the body. Change to larger needle. With Charcoal, work 3 rounds increasing to 64 (72, 84, 72, 80) stitches evenly spaced on the second round. Keeping the last stitch (the "seam stitch") in Charcoal, work Panel 3 of Border 2 increasing 1 stitch in pattern on each side of the Charcoal seam stitch every 3rd (3rd, 3rd, 2nd, 2nd) round until you have 156 (168, 176, 200, 210) stitches total. Work until the sleeve measures 20½ (20, 19¾, 19¾, 19¾) inches. Bind off the seam stitch, and work back and forth for 17 rows. With Charcoal, make the facing that covers up the cut edge: purl 1 round, knit 7 rounds. Bind off.

FINISHING: Machine stitch and cut along the double-stranded purl stitches for armhole openings (see Finishing, page 134). Graft the shoulders and sew in the sleeves. The sleeves are sewn farther in on the body than on a regular drop shoulder sweater. Using Charcoal, and beginning at left back neck edge, pick up 18 (18, 24, 24, 24) stitches for left shoulder, 39 (39, 39, 41, 41) stitches for the front neck, 18 (18, 24, 24, 24) stitches for right shoulder, 39 (39, 39, 41, 41) stitches for the back neck. You have 114 (114, 126, 130, 130) stitches total. Knit 1 round, purl 1 round, then knit 8 rounds increasing 1 stitch at each corner on every round. Bind off. Sew all the facings to the wrong side. Weave all loose ends into the back of the fabric. Steam lightly.

MODEL 1

Border 1

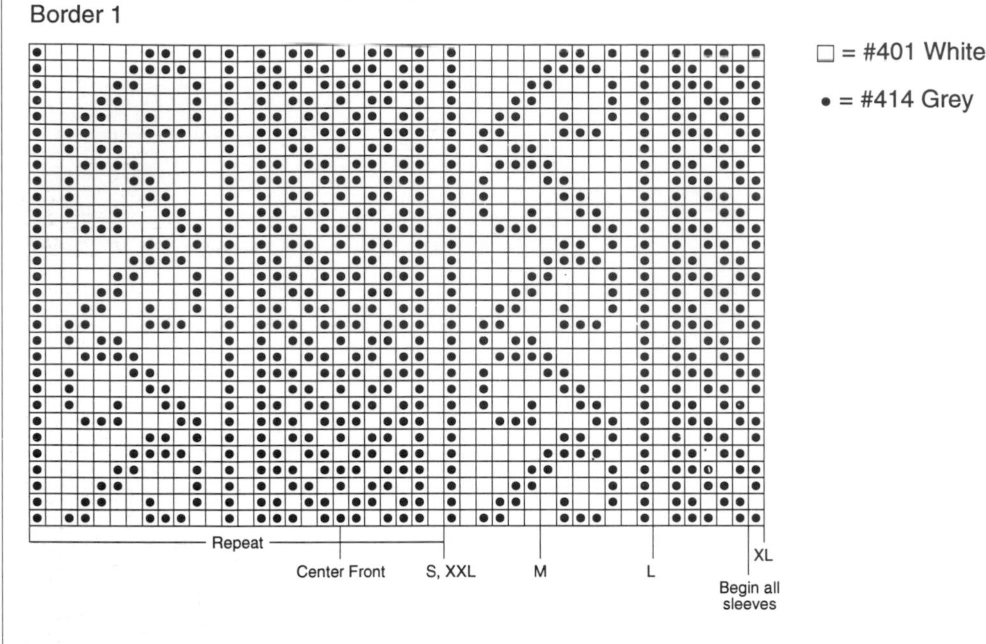

□ = #401 White

• = #414 Grey

Border 3

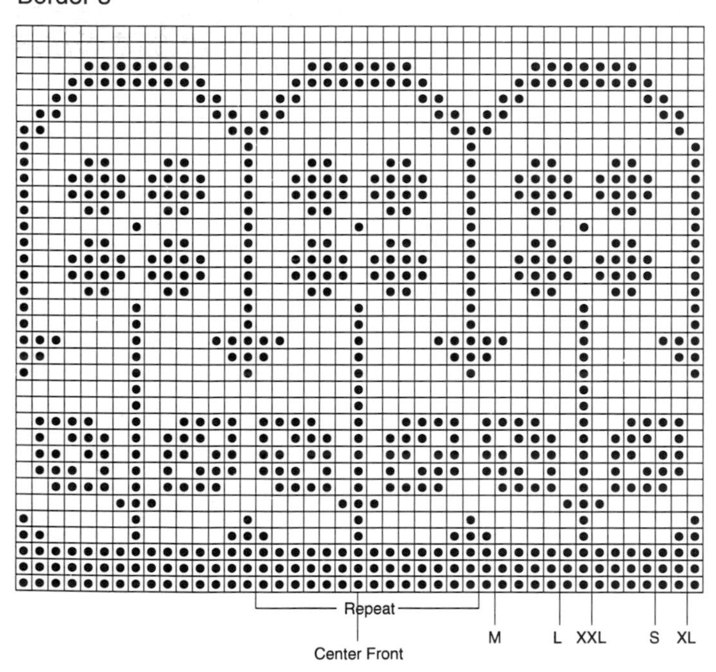

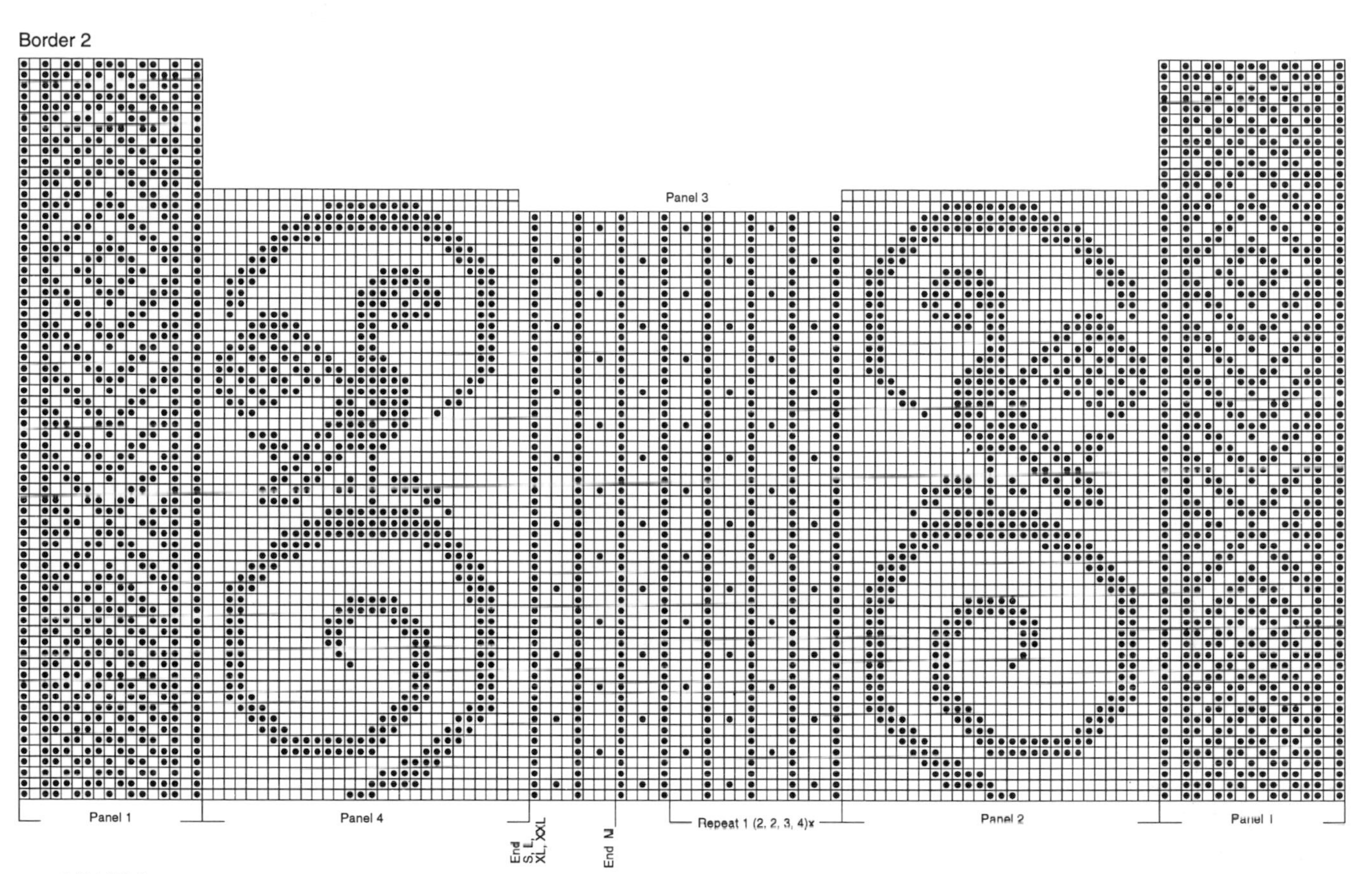

□ = #401 White

• = #414 Grey

MOTIFS

We have done the most unbelievable, impractical, and time-consuming experiments possible working with two- (or more) colored motifs. So we have no business telling people not to try to make a sweater with huge motifs and ten colors in a row. The important thing to ask yourself is: Do I believe that the final result will justify all the extra work? Or would it better to use another technique?

Two-colored designs were traditionally an effective way to combine the beautiful with the practical. Consider a mitten from Selbu, Norway, or a sweater from Setesdal. The garments were uncomplicated to knit, and it was seldom necessary to carry strands over more than five to seven stitches on the back. By knitting a two-colored pattern, the garment became twice as thick, twice as warm, and twice as interesting as a one-colored one.

It was easy to know when the fingers were long enough on a glove from Selbu, as the patterns were adjusted to each finger. Also, it was easy to see where increases should be on a sweater from Setesdal, as long as it had a border at the bottom, lice in the middle, and borders at the top.

Old-fashioned ski stockings had a separate design for the decreases below the calf, the heel, under the foot, and the toes, so it was easy to see if a mistake was made. By following the design correctly, the stocking fitted nicely. There are few—if any—traditional knitting patterns based on large rec-

tangular motifs. Large diagonal motifs are more common. Small square motifs that are built up by 2 × 2 or 3 × 3 stitches are also common and they are often used to decorate the lower edge of a sweater body or sleeves.

A. This is one of the easiest motifs to make. Each motif consists of two horizontal and two vertical stitches. You can find the same checkerboard pattern in Model 8, where the motifs consist of 7 × 7 stitches with an X in each square. The motifs in this design can easily be made larger without giving you problems with stranding.

B. These motifs vary in width, and, therefore, create a more busy pattern. You can create many exciting variations by combining different-sized motifs.

C. This is one way of using diagonals. It might be a good idea to put a design inside the diamonds to prevent impractical stranding.

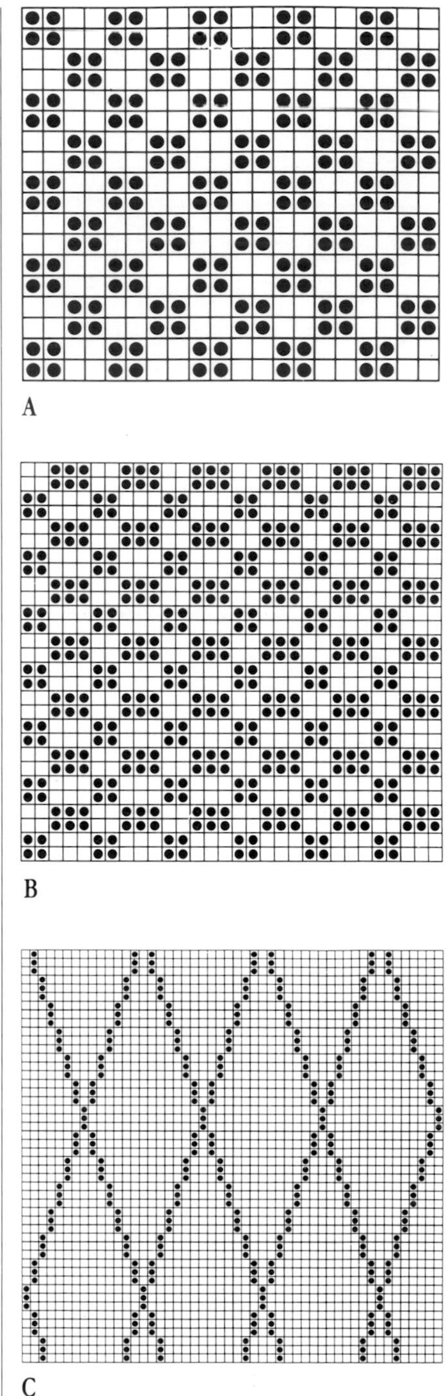

D. This net of small diagonals is built up like C, but because it is smaller, it is easier to knit. The design allows room for variety. You can embroider little designs in some of the motifs, fill every second row of motifs with a contrasting color, or play around with many different colors as you knit the main-color motifs. Model 14 shows another way of using diagonals in knitting the pair of tights. Half of each motif is knit using the contrast color, and the other half using the main color. Motifs like these invite you to play with colors. Model 6 (tights) divides the diagonals lengthwise to give a positive-negative effect. In addition, the borders are separated or tightened up by stripes between each motif.

E. and F. By framing the motifs, it seems as if there are three different colors, even though only two are used. You end up with light, dark, and varigated.

G. This is actually an arrangement of diagonal motifs, but they combine to form a leaf design.

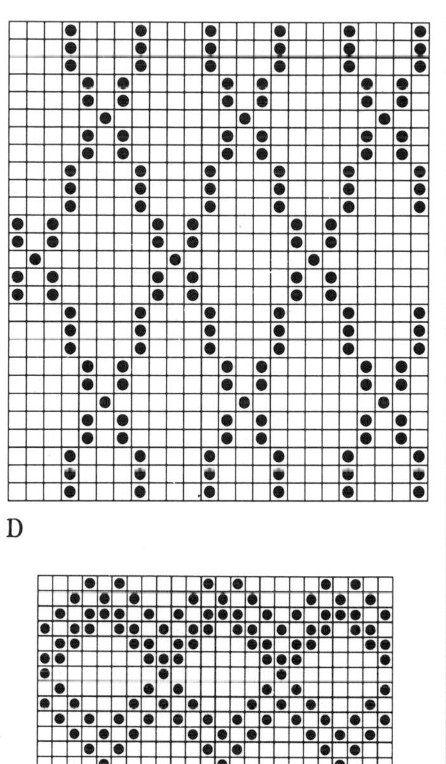

D

E

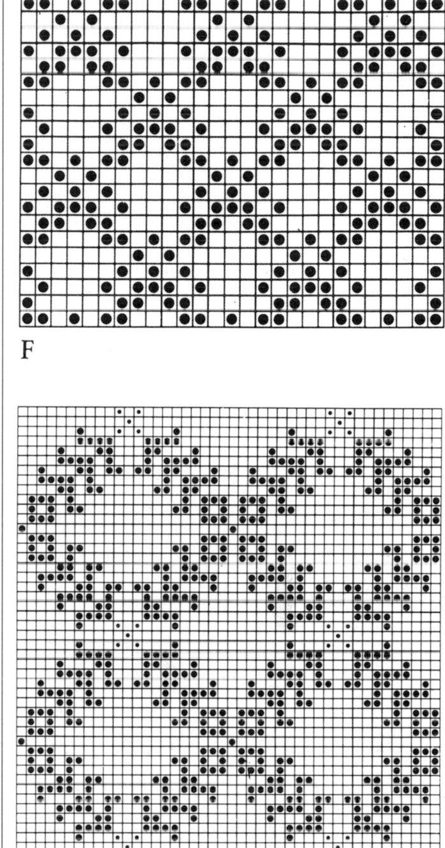

F

G

Try drawing a pattern consisting of repeated motifs. It is up to you to decide how large the motifs should be, and whether they should have horizontal and vertical lines or be slanted. First, make a couple of samples of each type and then experiment using the design that seems the most exciting.

e
b
c

ABOUT COLORS

A color's value is its appearence in different shades from light to dark. For example, red and blue are two different colors, but they can have the same value; that is, one can be as light or as dark as the other.

a. The swatch shows diagonal-shaped designs knitted in colors with about the same value. First, the motifs are knitted in bright yellow, green, blue, and red (A). Then, the same design is knitted in bright pastels (B). Finally, the same design is knitted in light pastels (C).

The same design has a different effect, depending on the values of the colors used. The pastels make the design seem cute and sweet. One variation makes the design seem free, easy, and fun, and another is reminicent of a clown's outfit.

In all three examples, there is a musical chord consisting of green, yellow, blue, and red, but all the different values give different impressions. It is important to think of the values as individual colors and not just as red, blue, yellow, and green. This will become more apparent in the following swatch.

b. This swatch is actually knitted in a triad of red, blue, and green, but there are six values of those colors: pinkish red, dark blue, light blue-green, light blue-red, light green-yellow, and light green. This is more interesting than if the swatch had been made up in only blue, red, and green.

c. The main impression of this swatch is that it is blue with horizontal purple stripes and very colorful. In addition to true blue, there are different values and hues of blue. Still, they go well together because there is one calm, but dominating color.

d. When we think of colors, we usually do not think of grey, beige, and brown, but rather colors such as pink, green, yellow, and turquoise. White and black are not considered colors, which is old news to anyone who has heard of primary colors or seen a circular color spectrum. Neither natural grey, natural brown, nor natural beige are considered actual colors. We tend to call them natural colors and associate them with Icelandic sweaters. But if you put those "colors" together, you will discover warm and cool "colors" among them, even though they are neutral. They have a tint of green, yellow, blue, or red. Combined with stronger colors they will die, but alone they will live their own poetic life.

e. The last swatch is a blend of yellow-red and blue-red colors combined with a calm medium blue. Many of the small dots connecting the squares have bright colors, but because there is very litttle of each color, it does not appear busy. It has been said that the color you have the least of is the color you notice the most. What do you notice most on this swatch? The yellow dots?

BORDERS AND SMALL DESIGNS

Dots, slanted and straight stripes, and motifs tighten a sweater's design. They follow certain rules, and it is easy to see how they are built up.

Before you continue on to a more complex design, it would be a good idea to try a smaller design. Divide a piece of graph paper into squares and draw designs as you think of them. It is fine to leave these designs open and half done. Make some copies and continue working on each copy. This will help you feel more free to experiment because you do not have to throw away all of your work if you are unhappy with one of the designs.

A. Try fitting small floral ornaments on 5 x 5 squares. Experiment. How much space should there be between each flower?

B. Different sized motifs are combined to create diagonal stripes.

C.Motifs with rounded corners create a honeycomb design. This is a good design to copy and continue working on.

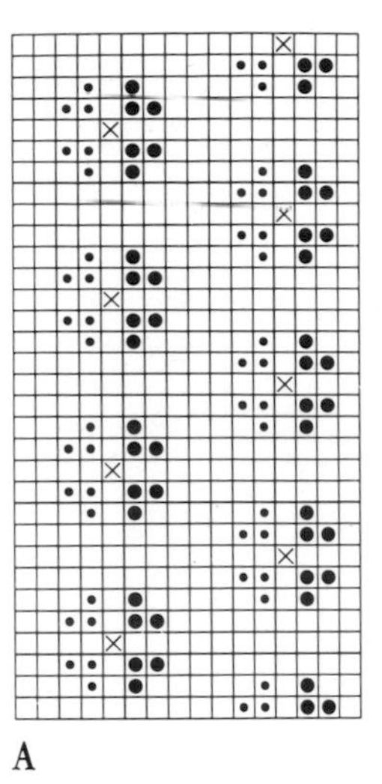
A

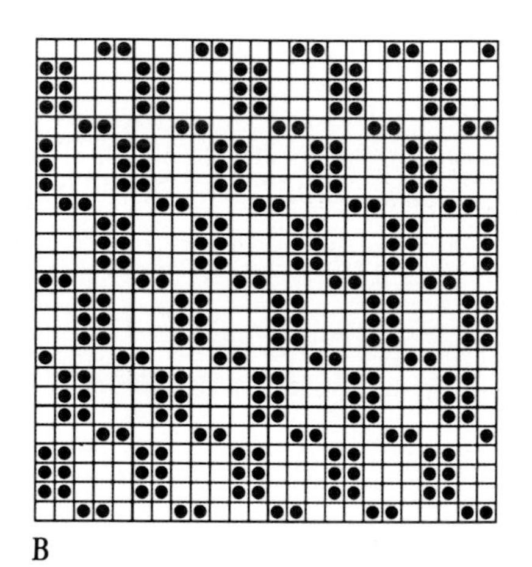
B

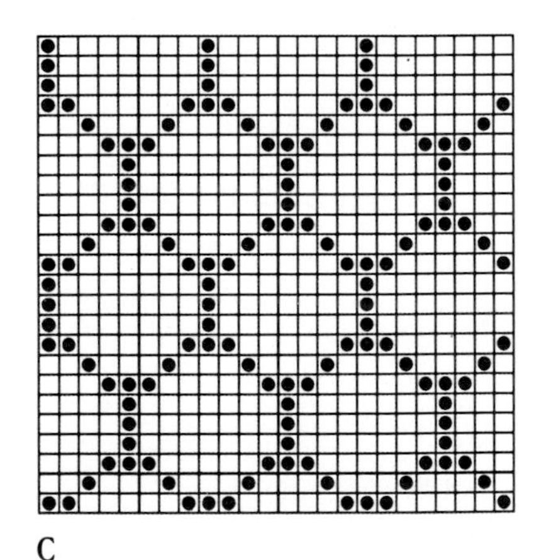
C

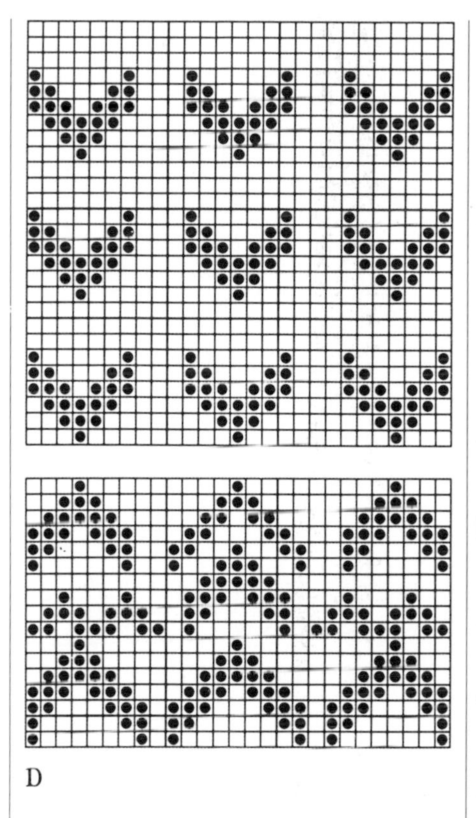

D

D. Vs in different variations and sizes create this pattern. Perhaps the bottom part could be used as an edge border, while the rest could serve as the main design on a garment.

e. Floral borders can be repeated on top of each other. These borders are actually stripes with flowers. One of the swatches is knitted using several different values of red, whereas the other is made with a combination of four strong pastels.

f. These "stripes" are made of tulips that are knit with strong colors, while the background is neutral. The effect is that the tulips come forward and become even more intense.

PART II
COMBINED DESIGNS

"THE DESIGN MACHINE"

In bright moments of inspiration, a design with color and flare can form in your head, and all you have to do is find your knitting needles and get started. You hardly have time to sketch the borders or even write down the pattern! However, you can not trust inspiration to show up when you need it the most.

In between those bright moments, the only thing that will do is hard work, especially if you want to develop your skills. In this case, "the design machine"—as we call this technique—will come in handy.

Start by making 7 × 7-stitch squares on graph paper using a sharp pencil. Make sure you space one row of squares between each "block" of squares. You can also make smaller blocks such as 3 × 3 or 5 × 5 if you want to work with smaller repeats. In the top row of blocks, make small designs of your own choice. Each design is to be made only once. It does not have to be symmetrical—it can start in one corner, or fill only half the block.

The next two rows of squares should be used for larger repeats: 15 × 15-stitch squares. Each repeat consists of four blocks of 7 × 7 stitches, with an open row between blocks, creating a center axis of the design. By the same principle, you can make even larger repeats such as 23 squares (3 × 3 blocks) or 31 squares (4 × 4 blocks).

Because all the repeats use the same number of stitches, it is possible to combine the designs going in all directions. Make a design in each of the large blocks as well. Now make eight to ten copies of your sheet, making sure you have plenty of extra sheets. Cut out all the repeats, but do not include the open spaces in between them. Place the repeats together with an open row of squares between each repeat. Switch and turn, combining repeats of several sizes. In other words, play around until you find designs that you like.

Glue the designs on graph paper, remembering to leave an extra row of squares between each block if the design is to be used with other repeats that are either bigger or smaller.

With the "design machine" you can make designs in many combinations. When you do not have to have everything planned out ahead of time, you feel more free, and it is easier to discover new possibilities as you proceed. Actually, you can find new designs in such play that could have a positive influence on your traditional designs.

A. This is one example of a design sheet that has been made by the "design machine" method.

A

B

C

B. The blocks of squares have been put together to make simple and more complex designs. In a few of these, the open row of squares is kept, or made part of the repeat. But in most of them, it has not been included.

C. This design, which is shown as two blocks of 15 × 15 in A (bottom right), forms 12 blocks. In this way, you can replicate the pattern and use it to develop a new, larger design.

D

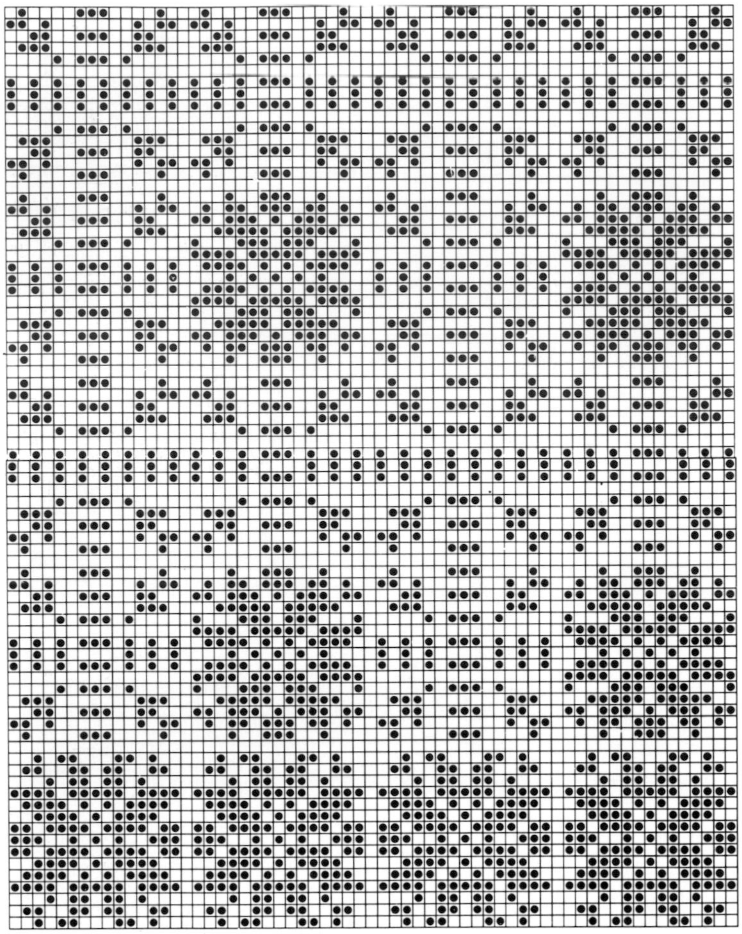

E

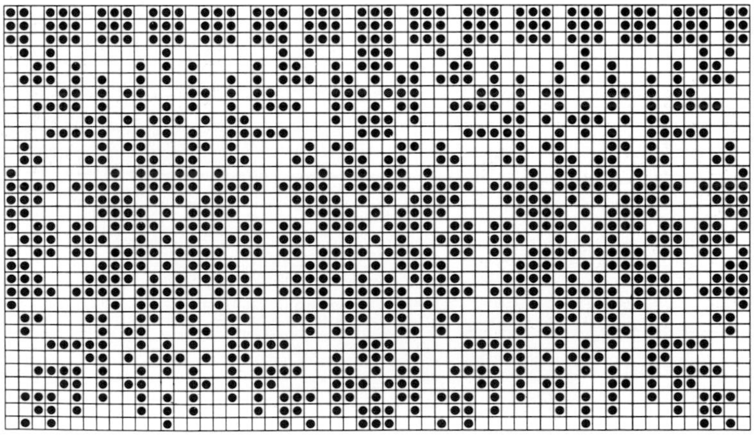

D. A variation of C. One element has been taken out, and the design has been supplemented with a star from A. The idea was to see how the weaving effect created by the stripes would function with a stronger design element. An edge border has been added with stars at the bottom.

E. The star has become the base for further experimentation. In this version, the star appears as an edge border with several different one-block elements above and below it. The way they are combined make them look like flowers.

In Models 11 and 12, the star has been used as the main motif with a lot of space around the design elements. A small one-block leaf creates a diagonal direction in the design. To further illustrate the possibilities of this method, we will include one more example—this one with only three design elements.

A and B. We start with two motifs of equal size.

C. On their own, they can make simple borders and main designs.

D. This design, appearing as diagonal lines, is made by combining the two elements in a checkerboard design.

E. Elements of the four designs are combined and placed in a checkerboard design. The sketch of arrows illustrates what directions the elements have.

F. Elements of the four designs are combined, but the B design is always going in the same direction. The sketch of arrows illustrates what direction the elements have.

A
B
C
D
E
F

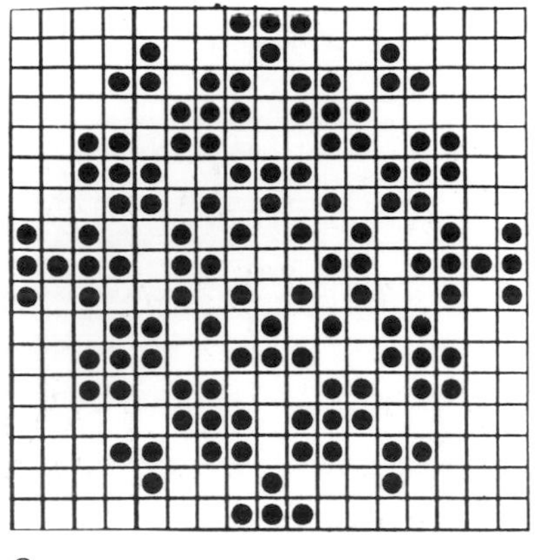

G

G. A new design element is added—a rose.

H. The rose is as big as four blocks of the A motif. This is why the two design elements combine nicely in a diagonal network. Notice how the large main design starts in the middle of the graph. Instead of splitting up the rose, several A designs are put side by side. In the bottom half, the rose and leaves are repeated and framed by two small, striped borders.

H

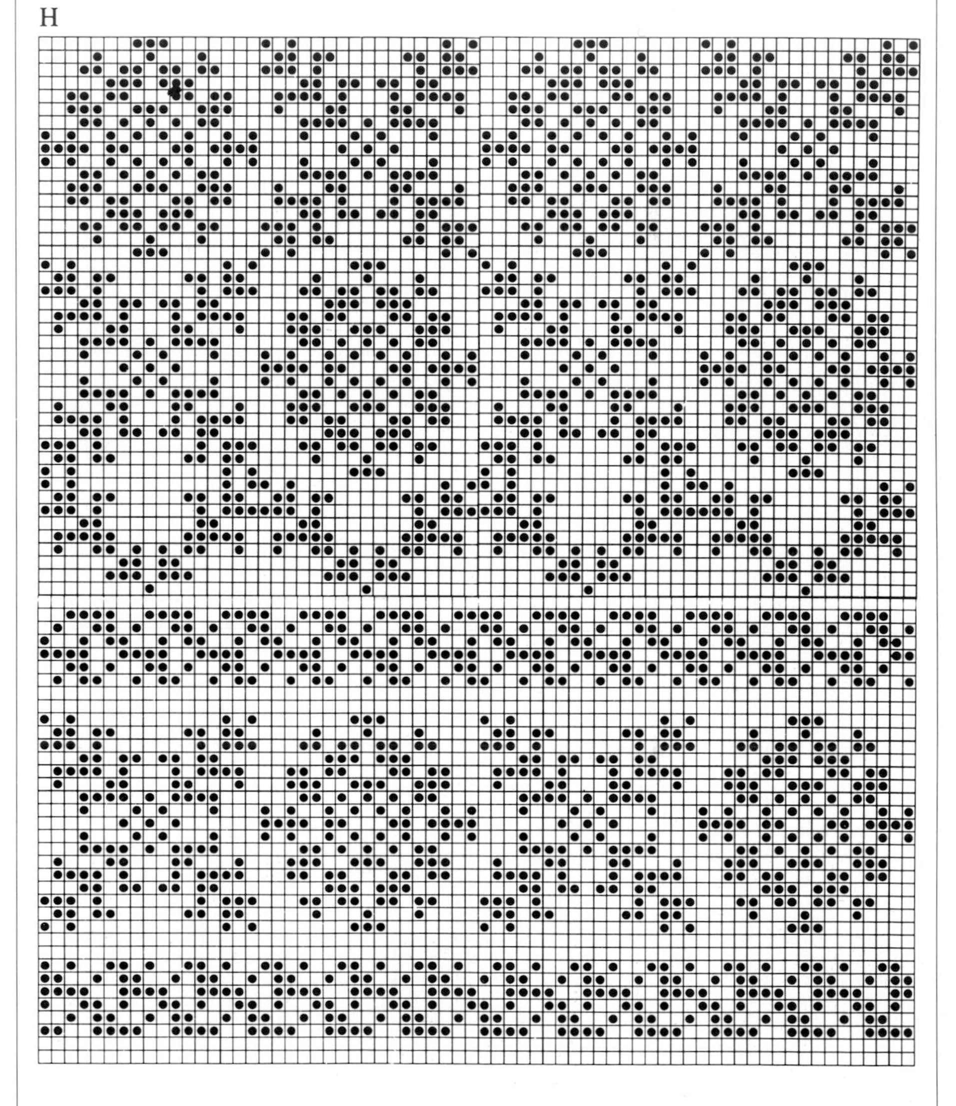

MODEL 2

PULLOVER WITH A MEDALLION DESIGN

The design on this pullover is made using the design machine. Because all of the pattern elements came out evenly (with the same repeat), it was easy to place a big medallion over the main pattern on the front and back of the pullover. Because it is difficult to increase in the main design on the body and sleeves, increases are worked into a striped design on each side of the body and under the sleeves. The stripes complement the big squares.

YARN: Rauma Finullgarn. The sweater shown is knit in the colors listed below.

CHART: page 43

SIZES: S (M, L)

COLORS: #449 Navy–400 (400, 450)g; #401 White–300 (300, 350)g

GAUGE: 27 stitches and 32 rounds = 4 × 4 inches

NEEDLE SUGGESTION: Circular and double-point knitting needles size 2.5mm and 3mm, or size necessary to obtain gauge. It is very important to knit to gauge otherwise the garment will be too big or too small.

BODY: Using smaller circular needle and Navy, cast on 248 (280, 312) stitches. Knit in the round for 8 rounds for the hem. Purl 1 round, and knit 8 rounds. Change to larger needle. In addition to the main pattern worked on the front and the back, the sweater has stripes on each side. The stripes consist of alternating 1 stitch of each color. These stitches originate by increasing 1 stitch on each side of the "seam stitches". Beginning the round at the left side seam with White (seam stitch), knit 6 stitches in stripe pattern, work 113 (129, 145) stitches of Border 1, 11 stitches in stripe pattern, 113 (129, 145) stitches of Border 1, then 5 stitches in stripe pattern. Continue to work Border 1 increasing 1 stitch in stripe pattern on each side of the seam stitches (4 stitches increased) every 4th round 10 times until you have 288 (320, 352) stitches total. Begin Border 2, the medallion, after the 5th (5th, 6th) repeat of Border 1. Armhole shaping starts after 7 completed squares. Bind off 27 stitches centered at each underarm. On the next round, cast on 2 stitches over the bound-off stitches. Purl these 2 stitches on every round using both strands of yarn. They are to be sewn and cut open for sleeve openings. You have 2 stripes left on each side of each arm opening. Work even. On last round of Border 2, bind off center front 47 stitches for neck opening. Cast on 2 stitches over the bound-off stitches and purl these stitches. Work one more square of Border 1. Work the same neck shaping on the back as you did for the front. Work another square of Border 1. Put the stitches on a holder.

SLEEVES: Using smaller double-point needles and Navy, cast on 51 (55, 57) stitches. Knit in the round. Work the hem as you did the body. Change to larger needles and increase to 66 (70, 78) stitches evenly spaced. Start the round with 1 Navy "seam stitch". Work Border 1 increasing 1 stitch in pattern on each side of the seam stitch every other row 2 (0, 8) times, every 4th round 33 (27, 34) times, then every 6th round 0 (6, 0) times. When you have completed 9 (9 1/2, 10) squares and have 136 (136, 162) stitches total, divide work. Bind off seam stitch and continue the design back and forth for 1 more square. To make the facing that covers up the cut edge, purl 1 round, knit 7 rounds. Bind off.

FINISHING: Machine stitch and cut along the double-stranded purl stitches for armhole openings (see Finishing, page 134). Graft the shoulders and sew in the sleeves. Using Navy, and beginning at left back neck edge, pick up 54 stitches for left shoulder, 47 stitches for front neck, 54 stitches for right shoulder, 47 stitches for back neck. You have 202 stitches. Knit 4 rounds decreasing 1 stitch at each corner every round. Purl 1 round, knit 4 rounds increasing 1 stitch at each corner. Bind off. Sew all the facings to the wrong side. Weave all loose ends into the back of the fabric. Steam lightly.

SKI HAT: Using Navy and larger double-point needles, cast on 144 stitches. Knit in the round for 1 1/4 inches for the hem. Purl 1 round, knit 2 rounds. Work 2 squares of Border 1. Beginning with Navy, alternate the two colors over the remaining stitches. Work until the hat measures 7 inches from the purl round. Pull the yarn through the stitches and gather. Fold the hem along the purl round and slip stitch to the purl side. Weave all loose ends into the back of the fabric. Steam lightly. Make a Navy pompom and sew it to the top.

MODEL 2

Border 2

Border 1
Repeat 5 (5, 6)x

S

L
M
S
Sleeve

Center
Body/Sleeve

L

M

End

□ = #401 White • = #449 Navy

MODEL 3

BLACK CARDIGAN WITH "LACE BORDERS"

This cardigan is inspired by the Setesdalskofte. We have interpreted this traditional sweater and given you similar lice and borders. The borders are built of irregular white dots on a black background and resemble lace. The edgings are black with narrow white stripes, and help to quiet down the main design. There is an embroidered acanthus border along the front bands.

YARN: Rauma Finullgarn. The sweater shown is knit in the colors listed below.

CHART: page 46

SIZES: S (M, L, XL)

COLORS: #436 Black–450 (500, 550, 600)g; #401 White–350 (400, 450, 500)g; #499 Light Burgundy–50 (50, 50, 50)g for embroidery; #489 Light Earth Green–50 (50, 50, 50)g for embroidery; #469 Red Orange–50 (50, 50, 50)g for embroidery; #431 Medium Gold–50 (50, 50, 50)g for embroidery

GAUGE: 27 stitches and 32 rounds = 4 × 4 inches

NEEDLE SUGGESTION: Circular and double-point knitting needles size 2.5mm and 3mm, or size necessary to obtain gauge. It is very important to knit to gauge otherwise the garment will be too big or too small.

BODY: Using smaller circular needle and Black, cast on 245 (277, 301, 333) stitches. Knit in the round. Purl the 4 center front stitches every round using both strands of yarn every pattern round. They are to be sewn and cut open for the front opening. Knit 7 rounds for the hem, purl 1 round, knit 5 rounds. Change to larger needle and work Border 1 for 2¾ inches. On first round of Border 2, increase or decrease to 244 (274, 304, 334) stitches. Work Border 2 until the cardigan measures 25½ (26½, 26½, 27¼) inches. Shape for the front neck by decreasing 1 stitch on each side of the purl stitches every round 3 (4, 4, 5) times total. When the cardigan measures 26½ (27¼, 27¼, 28) inches, bind off the center back 34 (37, 38, 43) stitches for the back neck. On the next round, cast on 3 new stitches over the bound-off stitches and purl these stitches every round using both strands of yarn. Continue working in the round, and at the same time decrease 1 stitch on each side of the back neck purl stitches every round 3 times. Work until the cardigan measures 27¼ (28, 28, 28¾) inches. Using Black, knit 1 round and bind off loosely.

SLEEVES: Using smaller double-point needles and Black, cast on 52 (52, 52, 56) stitches. Knit in the round, and make the hem as you did the body, increasing to 61 stitches on last row. Change to larger needles and work Border 1. Start the round with 1 Black "seam stitch". Increase 1 stitch on each side of the seam stitch every 4th round. Knit as many rounds of Border 1 as on the body. Work Border 2 increasing 1 stitch on each side of the seam stitch every 2nd round until you have 161 (165, 169, 173) stitches. Knit the sleeve until it is 3½ (4, 4, 4) repeats long. Using Black, knit 1 round. To make the facing that covers up the cut edge, purl 1 round, knit 7 rounds. Bind off.

FINISHING: Machine stitch and cut along the double-stranded purl stitches for front and neck openings (see Finishing, page 134). Using Black and larger needles, pick up the same number of stitches along each front edge. Cast on 2 extra purl stitches at the upper and lower front edges (4 stitches total), so that you can knit in the round. Using Black, knit 10 rounds, then work Border 1. Make buttonholes on the right side on the 5th round of stripes. Each buttonhole goes over 7 stitches (between 3 stripes). There are 17 stitches between buttonholes. Place the lower buttonhole by the first white

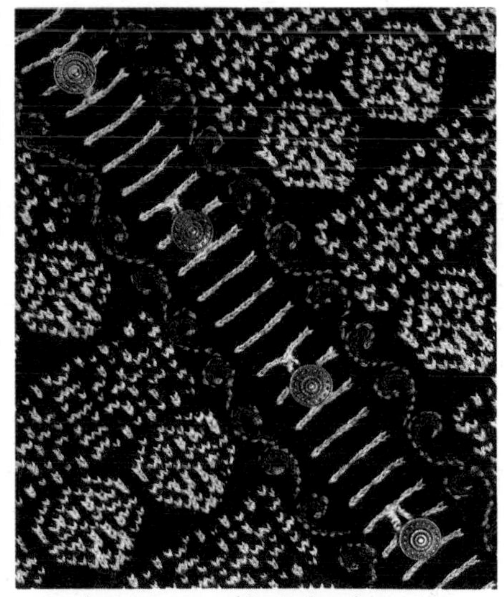

stripe (a minimum of 5 stitches from the edge). Bind off for buttonholes using White. On the next round, using White, cast on 7 stitches over the bound-off stitches. This way the buttonhole edges will be white, but the stitches black. Continue working stripes for another 5 rounds. Now, using Black, purl 1 round, then knit 5 rounds. Knit another round of buttonholes. Finish off by knitting 15 rounds. Bind off. Machine stitch and cut along the double-stranded purl stitches between the upper and lower edges of the front bands. Embroider on the front bands as shown in the detail photo. To work the stem stitch, pass the embroidery yarn over a knit stitch, pull it through to the purl side, go under the next knit stitch, and come up on the knit side. Then go back to the purl side in the same hole as the previous stitch ended. Make a chain stitch by coming up to the knit side and going down to the purl side in the same hole, leaving a loop on the knit side. When you make the next stitch coming up and going down in the same hole, make sure you also come up inside the loop you left on the knit side, and pull the thread.

Double up the buttonholes using buttonhole stitches. Each front goes over 3½ (4, 4½, 5) repeats measured from the front band. Mark the length of the sleeve opening, stitch and cut for the sleeve openings. Graft the shoulders. Using Black and larger needle, pick up stitches around the neck. Cast on 3 extra purl stitches at the center front so you can knit in the round. Purl these stitches on every round. Knit Border 1 stripes for 5 rounds. Make a horizontal buttonhole on the buttonhole side. Place it between 3 stripes 6 to 7 stitches from the edge. Knit stripes for another 5 rounds. Using Black, purl 1 round, then knit 5 rounds. Make a matching buttonhole. Finish off by knitting 5 rounds. Bind off. Sew 4 machine seams at the center front and cut open. Sew the corners from the purl side. Sew all the facings to the wrong side. Sew buttonhole stitches around the buttonholes. Sew in the sleeves. Weave all loose ends into the back of the fabric. Steam lightly. Sew on buttons.

MODEL 3

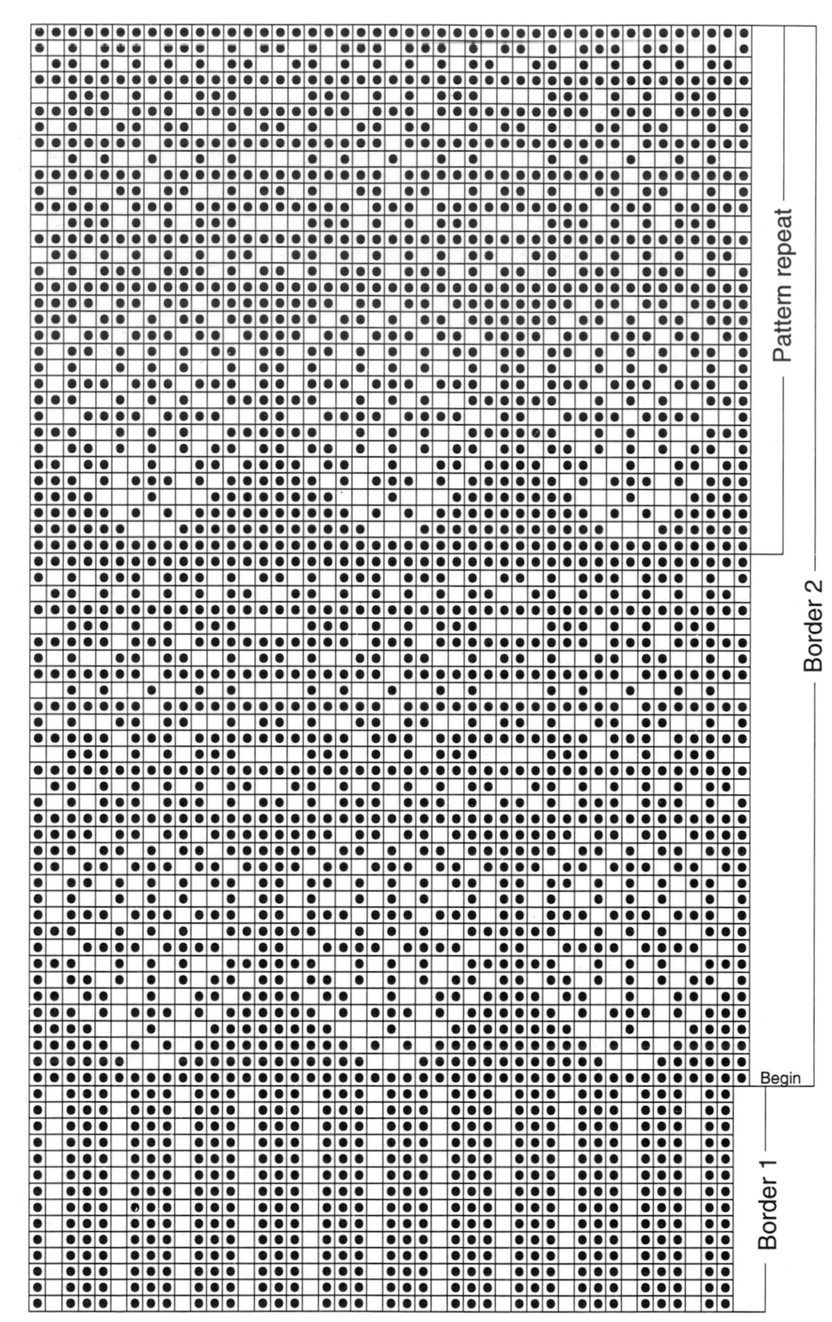

□ = #401 White

• = #436 Black

PLACING DESIGN ELEMENTS ON A SURFACE

The design machine helps you construct new designs. It is also fun to figure out how to use the same design element in as many ways as possible.

Find a design you like in your collection and make several copies of one of its elements. You can also cut elements into smaller parts and move them around in different configurations or remove parts of the original design. Glue together as many different variations as you can think of. When you are done, you might not recognize the design you started out with.

The basis for the following designs is the star in A. At first, it was glued together in the most obvious ways.

A. Stars are evenly placed on top of and next to one another.

B. Stars form a brick pattern.

C. Stars are used in a trellis design.

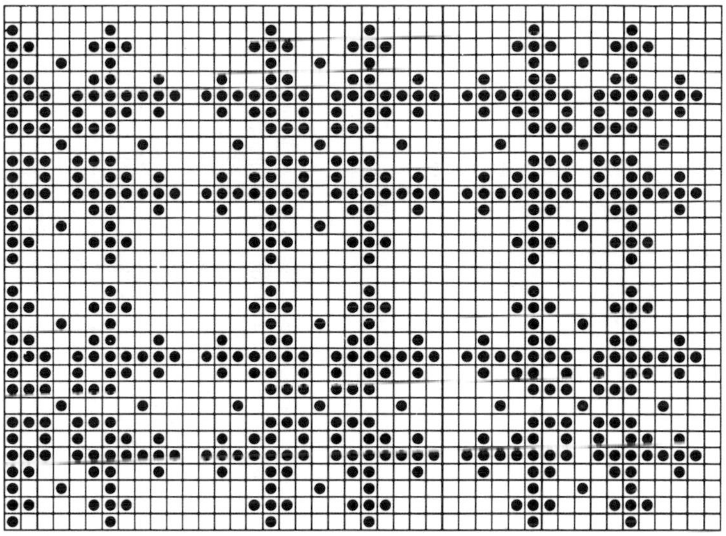

A

B

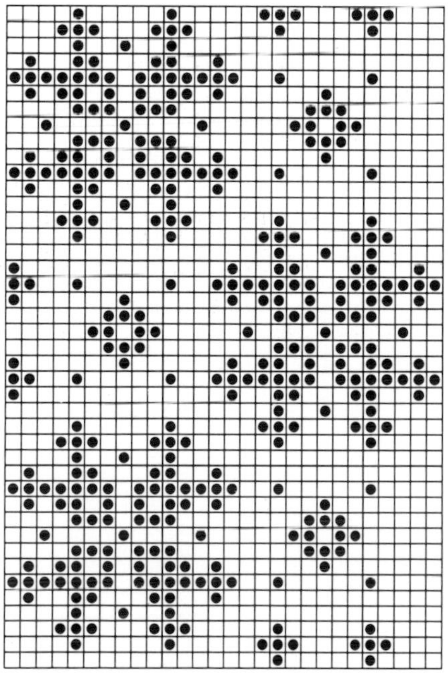

C

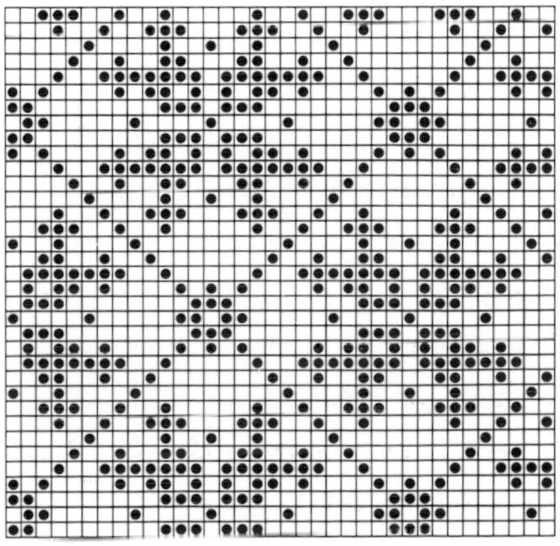

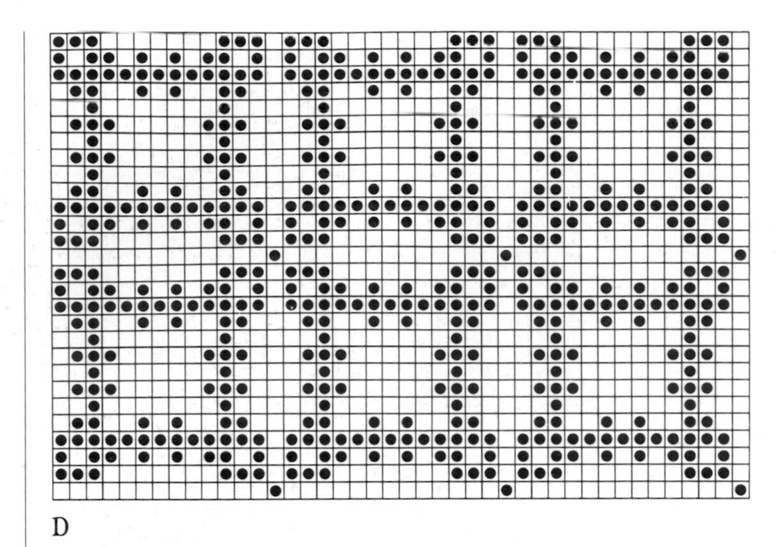

D

F

E

D. The stars are placed so close together in height and width that they look like boxes.

E. The stars are placed even closer together. They create a square design, and new shapes appear that are just as active as the star itself.

F. New "related" stars show up when elements from the original star are combined in different ways. These new stars are combined to form a diagonal design.

G. Here is another way of combining the stars.

H. Some of the design elements are developed further and put into patterns that have new forms in between them, forming a positive-negative design.

G

H

This is a good way to create variation, but at the same time achieve designs with certain similarities. Such related designs will work well together on a garment.

MIRRORS

Mirrors can help you see new possibilities in designs you have already made. If you use a pocket mirror as an axis placed next to part of a design—or a complete repeat of a design—you can see the design in reflection as you rotate it around the axis. With two mirrors placed together at right angles, the design fragments will create a quarter of a rosette. If you place the mirrors a little away from the design, you can see how the design appears as a repeat. It is worthwhile to transfer the designs you find in the mirror onto a new sheet of paper.

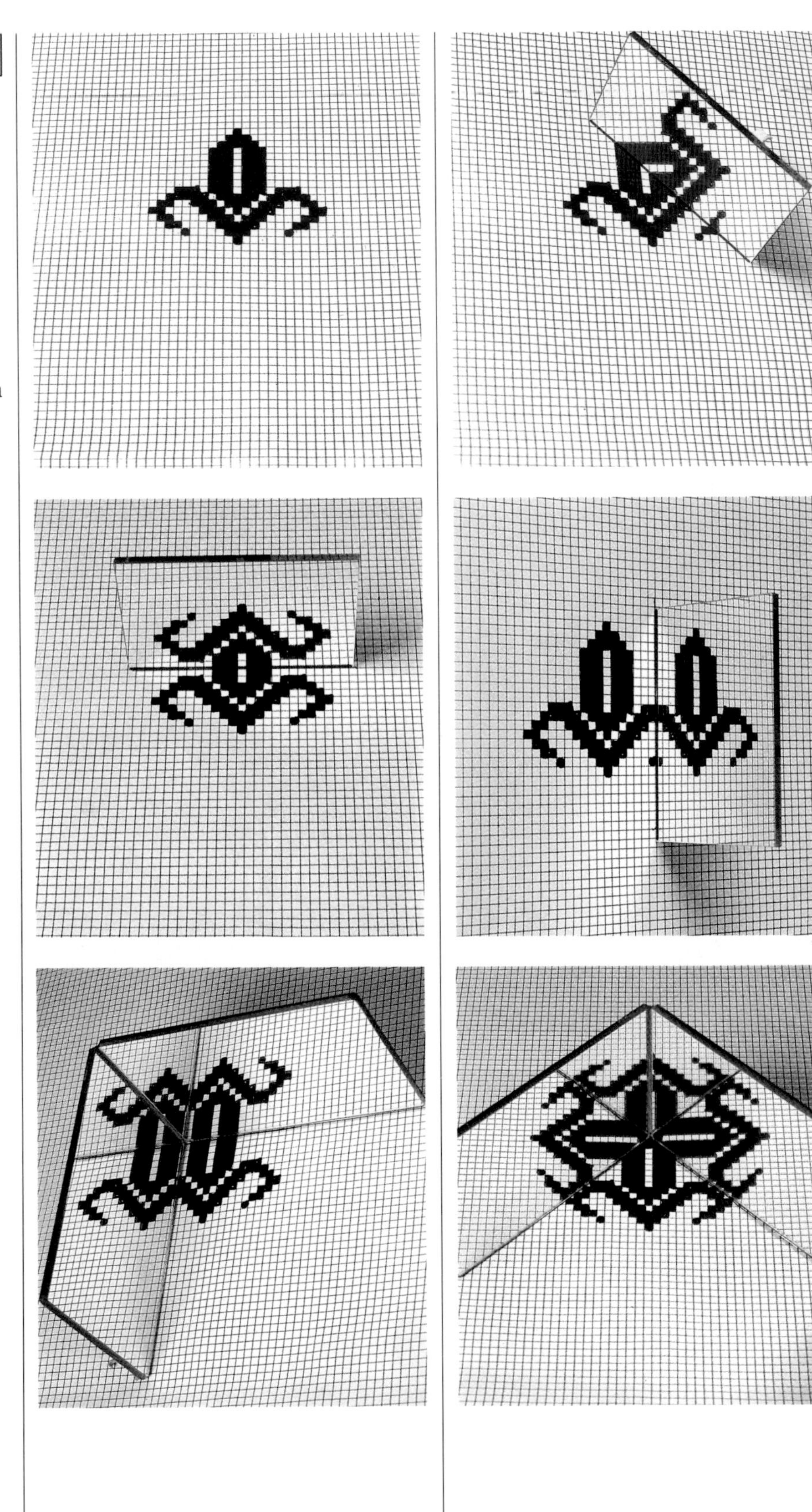

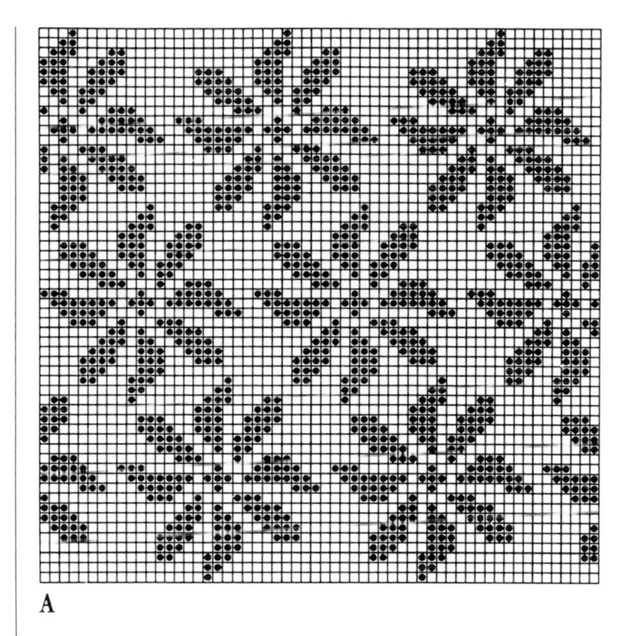

A. The flower works well as a basis for many mirror designs because it is not symmetrical. Here are several flowers placed evenly on graph paper.

B. The flowers are still evenly placed, but at a greater distance, with some leaves between them.

C. Here, we used two mirrors. One-fourth of the original flower is kept and repeated four times around the axis. The new flowers are then placed above and next to each other.

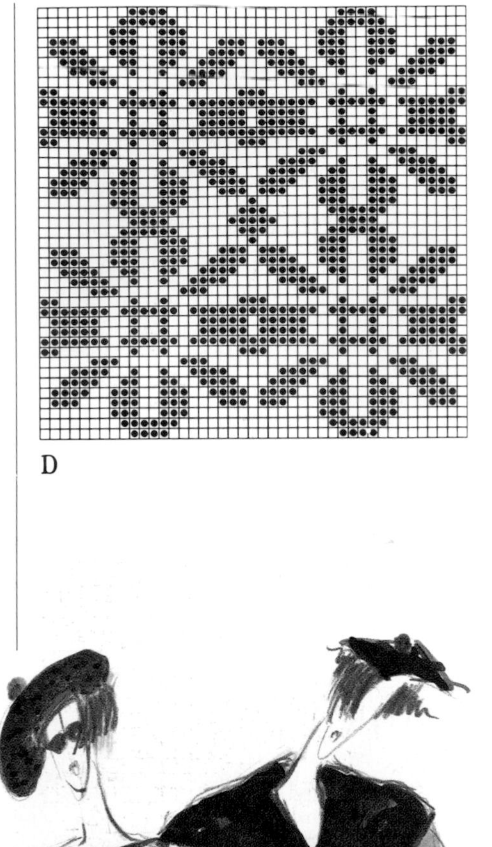

D

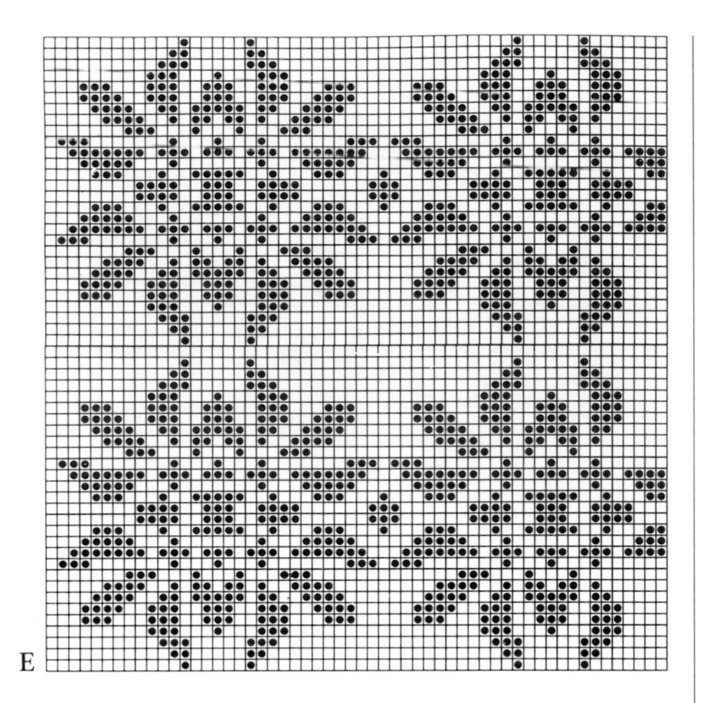

E

D. All the flowers are connected. It is becoming difficult to see that the design is actually made up of flowers.

E. With the help of the mirror, we have found yet another design element. The elements are, once again, placed evenly above and next to each other. They could also be placed in a brick design.

F. Each new round with mirrors leads to new discoveries and more polishing. This time, the design does not look much like the original flower.

F

VARIATIONS "OVER" A DESIGN

Until now, we have been busy trying to figure out how you can get the most out of one design element: by placing it on a surface in various ways, by cutting it into smaller elements, by repeatedly drawing it, or by using mirrors to make new designs from old ones. Now we will use two elements that are related, but not the same. By using them together, we can create many beautiful designs.

A. These two flowers look alike, even though they are made differently. They have "ornamental similarities", meaning that the lines and the dimensions indicate that they belong together. Technically, the flower to the left is a symmetrical design, while the flower to the right is a diagonal design. In Model 4, only the diagonal flower is used. The flowers are combined in striped borders on top of each other, with every second border acting as a reflection of the row below it. It looks as if the flowers are spread over the surface. If all the flowers were to face the same direction, they would make slanted lines.

B. The diagonal flower and its reflection are combined in pairs in a brick design. Together they make a symmetrical design element.

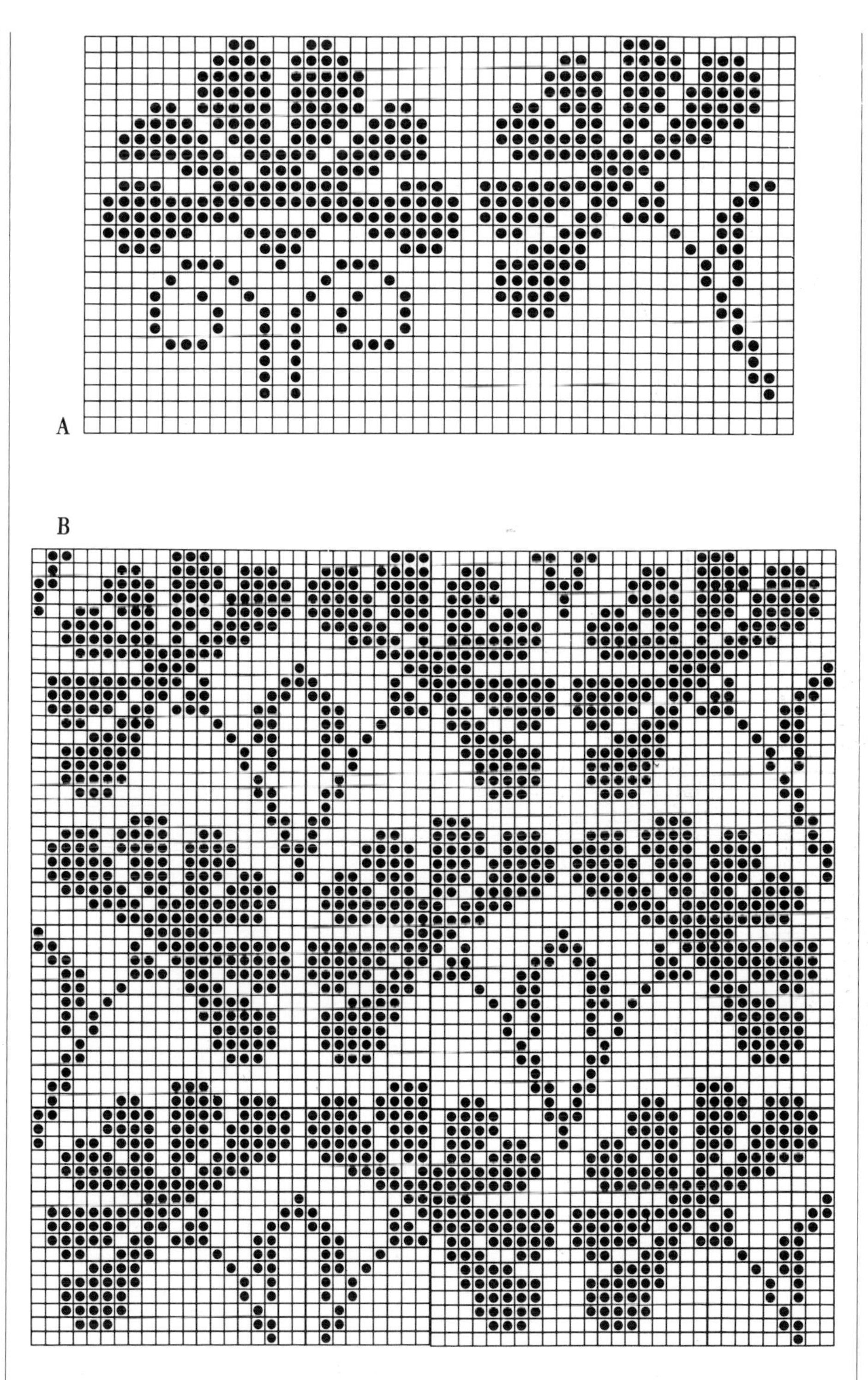

C. This design is comprised of the symmetrical flower only. The flowers are arranged to create vertical stripes in a brick design. The symmetrical flower has been given new, larger leaves in Model 5, Border 1. All the flowers are placed right above each other. In Border 2, the diagonal and the symmetrical flowers are used together. The design is divided by stripes, with the symmetrical flowers forming the center and the diagonal flowers forming the rest of the design.

To mirror a design

It can be quite time consuming to mirror design repeats. You have to be extremely accurate when counting them. Also, it is hard to see the squares upside down in your head before you put them down on paper. It is much quicker to use a copier to make a transparency on 8 1/2 inches × 11 inches clear film. Copy the design onto the clear film and then turn the film so that the "wrong" side faces down. Now make a paper copy, which will show the design as a reflection.

Ornamental design elements are used in the following two different cardigans. In Model 4a, the diagonal flower forms the main design, in contrast to a more detailed and ordered floral border. Both cardigans have lacy ruffled edges. In Model 5, the vertical design appears to add length to the flared "skirt".

The cardigans give completely different impressions, even though they are related designs. This is due partly to the different color choices, but it is also because each of the cardigans have their own personal style.

C

MODEL 4a

SHORT CARDIGAN WITH SHAWL COLLAR AND RUFFLE EDGE

This cardigan has blue, yellow, and green on the collar, and black, red, and two other yellow and green colors on the body and sleeves. Both the blue and the black are very dark and complement the other colors.

YARN: Rauma Finullgarn. The sweater shown is knit in the colors listed below.

Black seed beads

CHART: page 58

SIZES: S (M/L)

COLORS: #439 Red–400 (400)g; #431 Medium Gold–150 (150)g; #430 Green–150 (150)g; #436 Black–100 (100)g; #482 Dark Blue–100 (100)g; #493 Light Sage Green–50 (50)g; #450 Yellow Gold–50 (50)g

GAUGE: 27 stitches and 32 rounds = 4 × 4 inches

NEEDLE SUGGESTION: Circular and double-point knitting needles size 3mm, or size necessary to obtain gauge. It is very important to knit to gauge otherwise the garment will be too big or too small.

BODY: The cardigan is worked from the neck down. Using the circular needle and Red, cast on 217 stitches. Knit in the round. Purl the 3 center front stitches on every round using both strands of yarn. They are to be sewn and cut open for the front opening. Work 2 pattern repeats, purl 2 stitches for sleeve opening using both strands, 6 pattern repeats, purl 2 stitches using both strands, then 2 pattern repeats. Work according to the graph alternating 1 Medium Gold and 1 Green flower. Work until the cardigan measures 12¼ inches. Bind off the 2 purl stitches at each armhole. On the next round, cast on 21 (42) new stitches over both sets of bound-off stitches. You now get 12 (14) pattern repeats around. Continue knitting through the 7th (8th) repeat of flowers. Using Black, make the ruffle edge as follows:

Round 1: Knit around.

Round 2: *Knit 2 together, knit 4, yarn over*. Repeat between *'s around.

Round 3: Knit, knitting 1 and purling 1 stitch in each yarn over of previous round.

Round 4: *Knit 2 together, knit 3, yarn over, knit 2 together, yarn over*. Repeat between *'s around.

Round 5: As round 3.

Round 6: *Knit 2 together, knit 2, yarn over, knit 2 together, knit 3, yarn over*. Repeat between *'s around.

Round 7: As round 3.

Round 8: *Knit 2 together, knit 1, yarn over, knit 2 together, knit 6, yarn over*. Repeat between *'s around.

Round 9: As round 3.

Round 10: *Knit 2 together, yarn over, knit 2 together, knit 9, yarn over*. Repeat between *'s around.

Round 11: As round 3.

Round 12: *Knit 2 together, knit 13, yarn over*. Repeat between *'s around.

Round 13: Purl, then bind off as purl.

SLEEVES: The sleeves are knit from the shoulder down. Using circular needle and Red, cast on 168 stitches. Work reverse stockinette stitch back and forth for 6 rows for the facing (to cover up the cut edge later on), then work 12 (25) rows according to the Border 1 in stockinette stitch. Join and knit in the round, continue Border 1, and decrease 2 stitches (1 at the beginning and 1 at the end of the round) every 3rd round until you have 68 stitches left. Change to double-point needles when needed. Work until the sleeve measures 16½ inches from where you joined. Knit Border 2. Using Dark Blue, knit 2 rounds, purl 1 round, knit 8 rounds for the hem. Bind off. Sew all the facings to the wrong side. Weave all loose ends into the back of the fabric. Steam lightly.

COLLAR/FINISHING: Machine stitch and cut open for the center front and sleeve openings (see Finishing, page 134). Graft the shoulders. Using Dark Blue, pick up stitches along the left and the right front edges and around the back neck. Cast on 2 stitches at the lower edge and purl these stitches every round using both strands of yarn. They are to be sewn and cut open later. Knit Border 2. Using Dark Blue, knit 2 rounds, purl 1 round, then knit 29 rounds for the collar facing. Bind off. Machine stitch and cut along the double-stranded purl stitches along the front opening. Sew the corners to the purl side and hem the collar. Sew in the sleeves. Sew all the facings to the wrong side. Weave all loose ends into the back of the fabric. Steam lightly. Sew on the beads as shown in the detail photo.

MODEL 4b

TIGHTS FOR SHORT CARDIGAN

YARN: Rauma Finullgarn. The tights shown are knit in the colors listed below.

Black seed beads

SIZES: S (M, L)

COLORS: #439 Red–300g; #431 Medium Gold–50g; #430 Green–50g; #436 Black–150g

GAUGE: 27 stitches and 32 rounds = 4 × 4 inches

NEEDLE SUGGESTION: Circular and double-point knitting needles size 3mm, or size necessary to obtain gauge. It is very important to knit to gauge otherwise the garment will be too big or too small.

TIGHTS: Using double-point needles and Red, cast on 59 (63, 65) stitches for one leg. Knit in the round. Knit Border 4, increasing 1 stitch on each side of the inseam (the first and last stitch of the round) of the leg every 5th round. Upon completion of Border 4, work Border 3 until you have 147 (151, 159) stitches. Knit until the leg measures 27 1/4 (28, 28 3/4) inches. Knit the other leg to match.

Bind off 15 stitches at the inseam of each leg (the center stitch and 7 stitches to each side). Put the two legs together, the inseams with the bound-off stitches facing each other. Put all the stitches from both legs on a circular needle. Continue Border 3, knitting in the round. At the same time, decrease at the center front and the center back as follows: At the front, decrease 2 stitches every other round (1 stitch from each leg). Repeat 3 times for a total of 8 stitches decreased. At the back, decrease 2 stitches every other round 10 times for a total of 20 stitches decreased. Then knit even until the tights measures 37 3/4 (38 1/2, 39 1/2) inches. Using Black, knit for 1 1/4 inches (waist band), purl 1 round, knit for 1 1/4 inches, and bind off. Fold the waist band at the purl round to make a casing for elastic. Sew the crotch seam.

Using Black, knit a ruffle on each leg: Pick up 66 stitches.

Round 1: Knit.

Round 2: *Knit 2 together, knit 4, yarn over*. Repeat between *'s around.

Round 3: Knit, knitting 1 and purling 1 stitch in each yarn over of the previous round.

Round 4: *Knit 2 together, knit 3, yarn over, knit 2 together, yarn over*. Repeat between *'s around.

Round 5: As round 3.

Round 6: *Knit 2 together, knit 2, yarn over, knit 2 together, knit 3, yarn over*. Repeat between *'s around.

Round 7: As round 3.

Round 8: *Knit 2 together, knit 1, yarn over, knit 2 together, knit 6, yarn over*. Repeat between *'s around.

Round 9: As round 3.

Round 10: *Knit 2 together, yarn over, knit 2 together, knit 9, yarn over*. Repeat between *'s around.

Round 11: As round 3.

Round 12: *Knit 2 together, knit 13, yarn over*. Repeat between *'s around.

Round 13: Purl.

Bind off as purl. Sew beads on the flower borders.

BERET: Using smaller circular needle and Black, cast on 148 stitches. Knit in the round for 1 1/4 inches for the hem. Next round: *Yarn over, knit 2 together*, repeat between *'s around. Knit 3/4 inch. Decrease 1 stitch. Change to Red and knit 1 Yellow Gold flower repeat according to Border 4. Change to larger needle and Black. Knit, and increase as follows: *Knit 4, increase 1*, repeat between *'s around. Knit 6 rounds. Next round: *Knit 5, increase 1*, repeat between *'s around. Knit 6 rounds. Purl 1 round, knit 6 rounds. Now decrease as follows:

Knit 5, decrease 1, repeat between *'s around. Knit 6 rounds.

Knit 4, decrease 1, repeat between *'s around. Knit 6 rounds.

Knit 3, decrease 1, repeat between *'s around. Knit 6 rounds.

Knit 2, decrease 1, repeat between *'s around. Knit 6 rounds.

Knit 1, decrease 1, repeat between *'s around.

Knit 2 together around, pull the yarn through remaining 19 stitches and gather. Sew all the facings to the wrong side. Weave all loose ends into the back of the fabric. Steam lightly. Make a small Green pompom and sew it to the top.

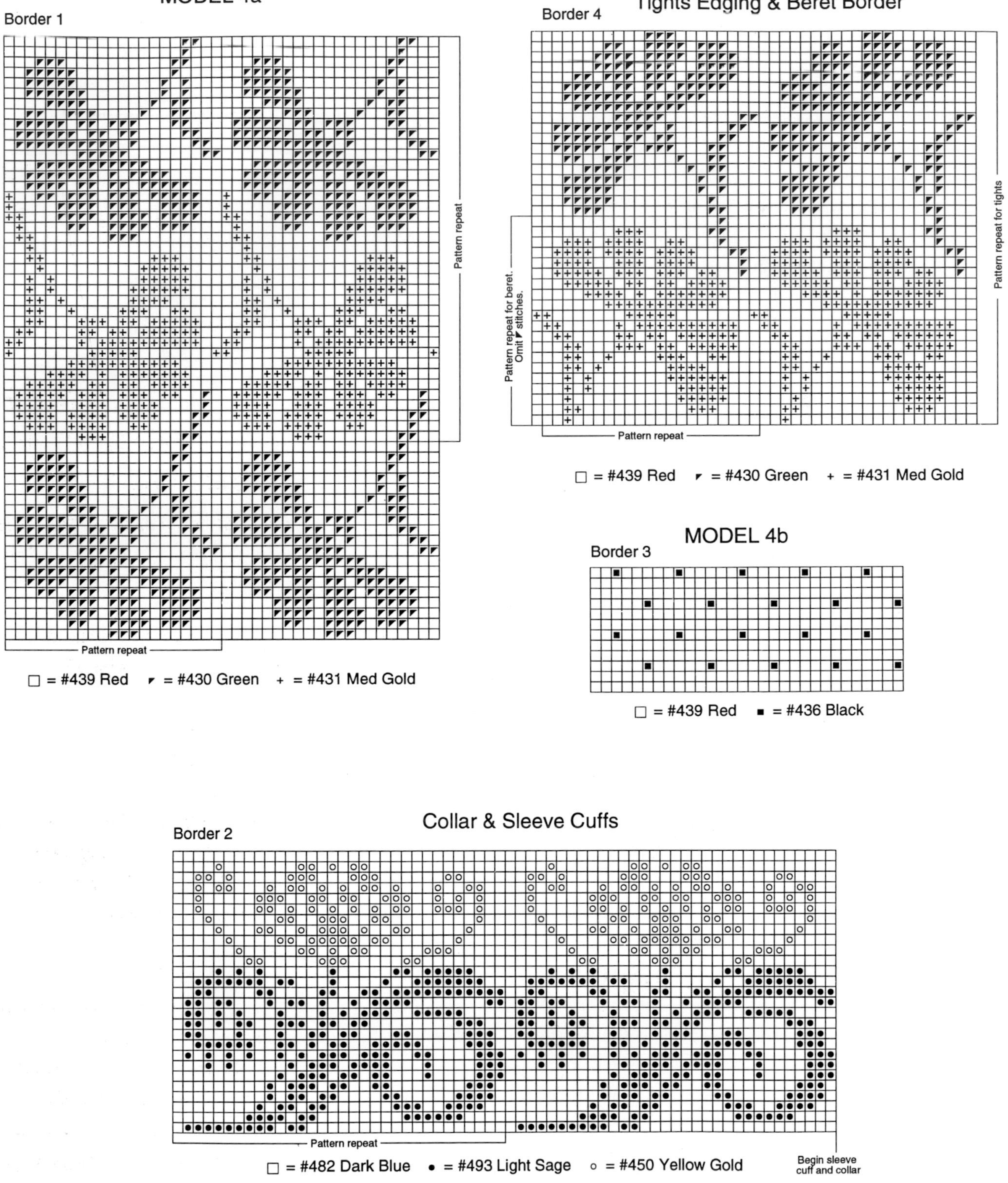
MODEL 4a
Border 1
Pattern repeat
Pattern repeat
□ = #439 Red ◤ = #430 Green + = #431 Med Gold
Tights Edging & Beret Border
Border 4
Pattern repeat for beret. Omit ◤ stitches.
Pattern repeat for tights
Pattern repeat
□ = #439 Red ◤ = #430 Green + = #431 Med Gold
MODEL 4b
Border 3
□ = #439 Red ■ = #436 Black
Collar & Sleeve Cuffs
Border 2
Pattern repeat
□ = #482 Dark Blue • = #493 Light Sage ○ = #450 Yellow Gold
Begin sleeve cuff and collar

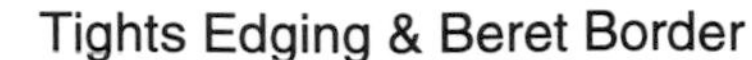

MODEL 5

FLARED CARDIGAN WITH YOKE

Here, the colors are used to underline the shape of the garment. The yoke has a different main color than the sleeves and the "skirt". The main color on the "skirt" is repeated in the beads sewn to the flowers on the yoke.

YARN: Rauma Finullgarn. The sweater shown is knit in the colors listed below.

Black seed beads

7 pewter clasps

CHART: page 61

SIZE: One size

COLORS: #455 Light Green–150g; #4886 Cyclamen–200g; #439 Red–200g; #469 Red Orange–200g; #4387 Dark Charcoal–350g

GAUGE: 27 stitches and 32 rounds = 4 × 4 inches

NEEDLE SUGGESTION: Circular and double-point knitting needles size 3mm, or size necessary to obtain gauge. It is very important to knit to gauge otherwise the garment will be too big or too small.

BODY: The cardigan is worked in the round from the neck down. Using circular needle and Light Green, cast on 295 stitches. Join and work Border 1 as follows: Knit 3 pattern repeats according to the graph, purl 2 stitches, knit 6 pattern repeats, purl 2 stitches, knit 3 pattern repeats, knit end stitch, and purl 2 stitches. Purl the purl stitches every round using both strands. They are to be sewn and cut open later on. After the 4th repeat of flowers, bind off the 2 purl stitches on each side, but keep purling the 2 center front stitches. Change to Dark Charcoal, and increase evenly spaced to 321 stitches. Starting at the center front, work as follows: Work Panel 1 of Border 2, work 4 repeats of Panel 2 of Border 2, work Border 4, work 4 repeats of Panel 2 of Border 2 omitting the last 3 stitches of the last repeat, work Panel 1 of Border 2, purl 2 front stitches. At the same time as you knit the borders, increase 1 stitch on each side of each of the 12 panels every 24th round (increases are shown on graph). Each panel will be wider, forming gussets. The increased stitches are worked in Dark Charcoal all the time. Increase until you have 417 stitches. Using Dark Charcoal, knit 2 rounds after the 5th row of flowers. Change to Light Green, and knit the ruffle:

Round 1: Knit.

Round 2: *Yarn over, knit 2 together*, repeat between *'s around.

Round 3: *Knit 1, (alternate 1 knit and 1 purl stitch) 3 times in each yarn over of the previous round.

Round 4: Knit.

Round 5: Purl.

Bind off.

SLEEVES: The sleeves are worked in the round from the shoulders down. Using circular needle and Dark Charcoal, cast on 163 stitches. Work reverse stockinette stitch back and forth for 6 rows for the facing (to cover up the cut edge later on). Work Border 3, and at the same time, decrease 2 stitches (1 at the beginning, and 1 at the end of the round) every other round until you have 63 stitches. Work until the sleeve measures 19 1/2 inches. Using Dark Charcoal, knit 2 rounds. Using Light Green, finish with a ruffle like on the body.

FINISHING: Machine stitch and cut along the double stranded purl stitches for armhole and neck openings (see Finishing, page 134). Baste, machine stitch and cut the neckline. This round neck extends 20 stitches to each side of the center front and the center back, is 4 inches deep at the center front, and 3/4 inch deep at the center back. Sew the shoulder seams. Using Dark Charcoal, pick up stitches along the front edges for the facing to cover the cut edge. Knit rows 1 and 2, then work stockinette stitch for 8 rows, and bind off. Using Dark Charcoal, work ruffles around the neck opening. Sew all the facings to the wrong side. Weave all loose ends into the back of the fabric. Steam lightly. The cardigan has clasps on the inside for closures. Sew the beads on the yoke as shown in the detail photo.

PILLBOX HAT

Using larger circular needle and Light Green, cast on 144 stitches. Knit in the round for 1 1/4 inches (for hem), purl 1 round, knit 2 rounds. Knit 1 repeat of Border 1 from the top of the graph to the bottom. Using Light Green, knit 3 rounds, purl 1 round, then decrease as follows:

Round 1: *Decrease 1, knit 6*, repeat between *'s around. Knit 6 rounds.

Next round: *Decrease 1, knit 5*, repeat between *'s around. Knit 5 rounds.

Next round: *Decrease 1, knit 4*, repeat between *'s around. Knit 4 rounds.

Next round: *Decrease 1, knit 3*, repeat between *'s around. Knit 3 rounds.

Next round: *Decrease 1, knit 2*, repeat between *'s around. Knit 2 rounds.

Next round: *Decrease 1, knit 1*, repeat between *'s around. Knit 1 round. On the next round, knit 2 together around, pull the yarn through the remaining stitches, and gather. Sew all the facings to the wrong side. Weave all loose ends into the back of the fabric. Steam lightly.

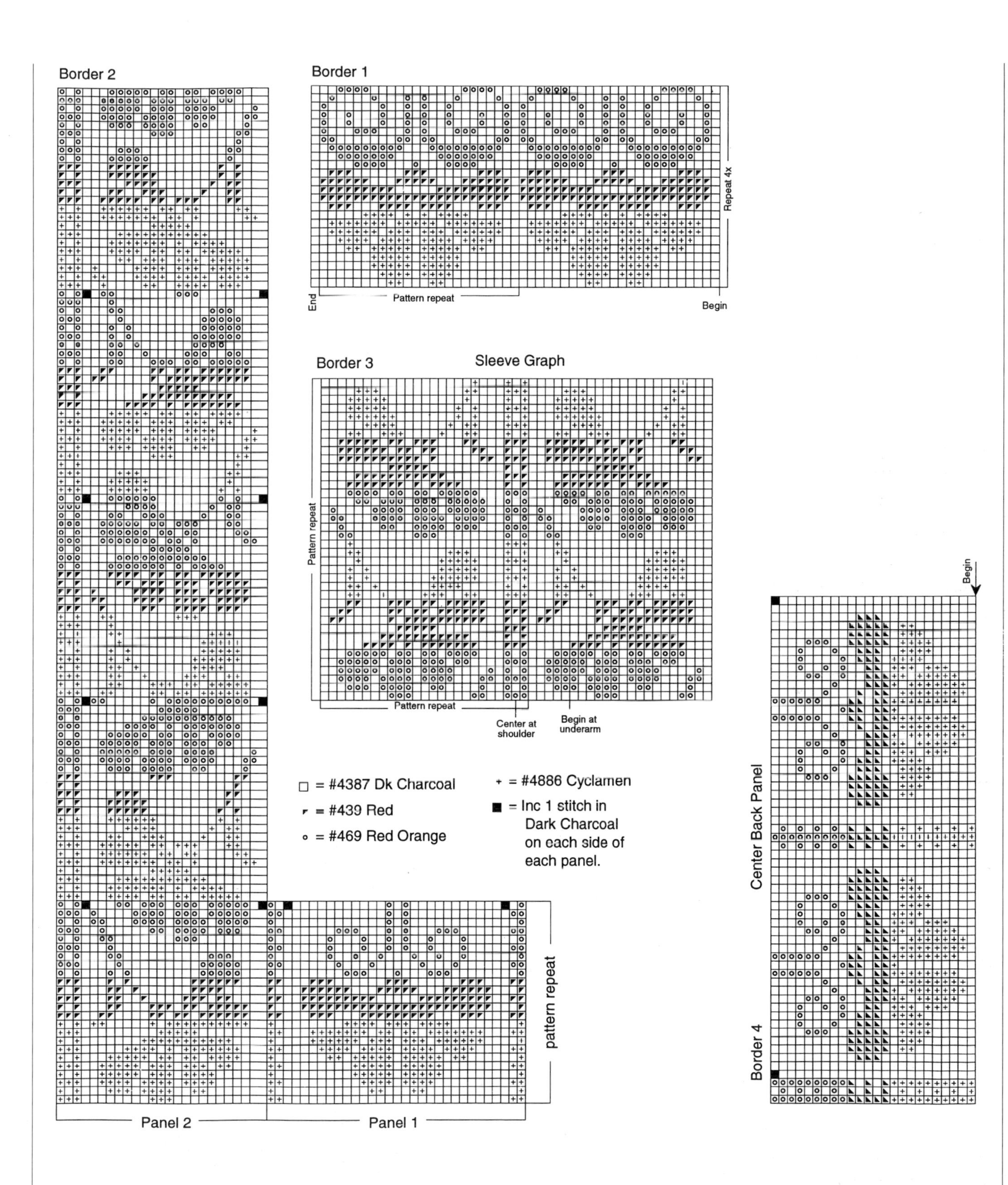
Border 2
Border 1
Repeat 4x
End
Pattern repeat
Begin
Border 3
Sleeve Graph
Pattern repeat
Pattern repeat
Center at shoulder
Begin at underarm
□ = #4387 Dk Charcoal
◤ = #439 Red
○ = #469 Red Orange
+ = #4886 Cyclamen
■ = Inc 1 stitch in Dark Charcoal on each side of each panel.
pattern repeat
Panel 2
Panel 1
Begin
Center Back Panel
Border 4

Positive-Negative

Another way to vary designs is to make them positive-negative where the main color in one square is the contrast color in the next square, and vice versa. Positive-negative designs can also be combined in different ways to create more variations. In Model 6, Border 2, a flower has been placed inside a white triangle (main color) with black squares (contrast color) and inside a black triangle with white squares. One of the triangles is placed upside down, and together the dark and the light triangle form a zigzag border.

Two similar looking designs are combined in a checkerboard design. One design has a light main color, and the other has a dark main color. Technically, this design is easy to knit, without long strands on the back. Visually, it has good contrast because the large repeats alternate between light and dark.

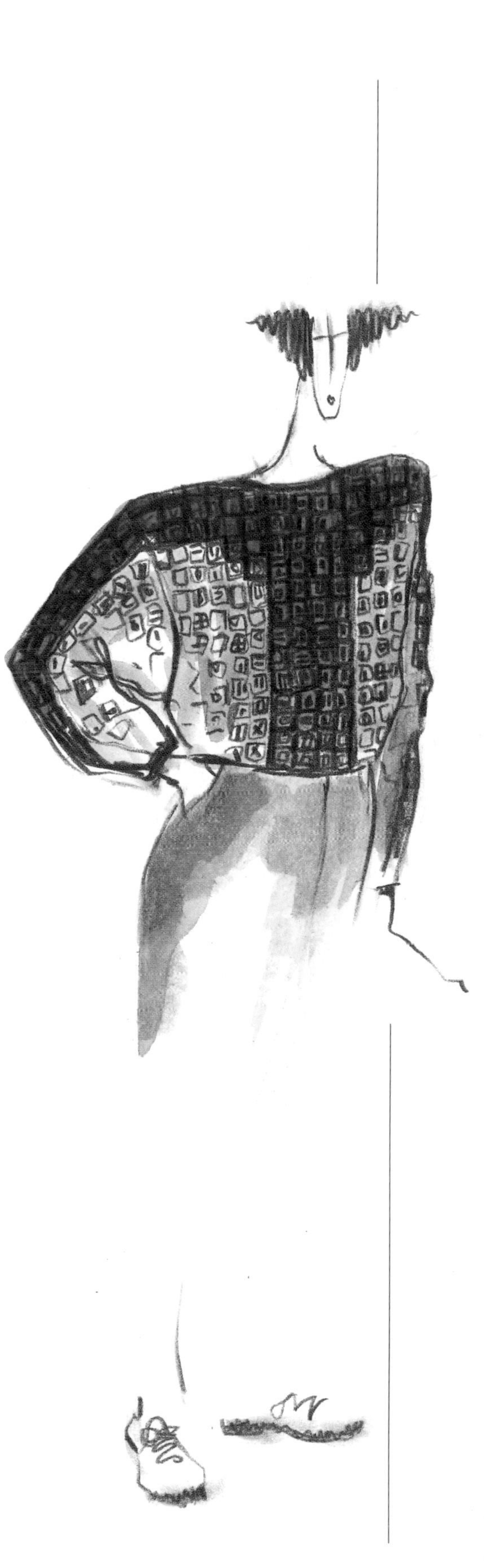

This is not the same motif being used in a positive-negative design, but in a leaf and flower design. The leaf is made on a light background, and the flower on a dark background. In this way, the color of the flowers works as the background for the leaves, and the color of the leaves works as the background for the flowers.

MODEL 6a

LONG PULLOVER WITH ZIGZAG BORDER AND TIGHTS WITH DIAMOND DESIGN

In this sweater, the zigzag border of flowers in a positive-negative effect is combined with a related surface design. Notice the effect of the zigzag border at the bottom of the sleeves. The borders look like cuffs, even though they are knitted in the traditional way.

The squares on the tights have a positive-negative design as well. This effect is not as strong, which is why it helps to tighten the large design on the sweater, even if the colors used are quite strong.

YARN: Rauma Finullgarn. The sweater shown is knit in the colors listed below.

CHARTS: pages 66 67

SIZES: S (M, L)

COLORS: #443 Dark Royal–250 (300, 300)g; #461 Orange–50g for all sizes; #4886 Cyclamen–150g for all sizes; #455 Light Green–50g for all sizes; #469 Red Orange–100g for all sizes; #439 Red–100g for all sizes; #498 Light Yellow Green–50g for all sizes; #489 Light Earth Green–50g for all sizes

GAUGE: 27 stitches and 32 rounds = 4 × 4 inches

NEEDLE SUGGESTION: Circular and double-point knitting needles size 3mm, or size necessary to obtain gauge. It is very important to knit to gauge otherwise the garment will be too big or too small.

BODY: Using circular needle and Dark Royal, cast on 272 (304, 336) stitches. Knit in the round for 8 rounds for the hem, and purl 1 round. Knit Border 1 increasing 0 (2, 4) stitches on last row. Work Border 2 decreasing 0 (2, 4) stitches on last row. Work Border 3, then increase evenly to 280 (320, 360) stitches. Work Border 4 as directed until you have 7 (8, 9) color changes. Decrease to 272 (304, 336) stitches. Finish with Border 5. Mark the 76 center front and center back stitches for the neck facing. Put the remaining stitches on holders. Using Dark Royal, put the 152 neck facing stitches on a circular needle. Purl 1 round, knit 8 rounds, and bind off.

SLEEVES: Using double-point needles and Dark Royal, cast on 48 (56, 56) stitches. Knit in the round. Knit the hem and Border 1 like the body. On the first round of Border 2, increase evenly to 64 (72, 72) stitches. Knit Borders 2 (center pattern as shown on the graph), 3, and 4 (center pattern as shown on the graph). At the same, time increase 2 stitches (1 stitch at the beginning, and 1 stitch at the end of the round) every 3rd round until you have 156 (168, 168) stitches. Knit until you have 5 color changes of Border 4. Finish with Border 5. To make the facing that covers up the cut edge: purl 1 round, knit 7 rounds, and bind off.

FINISHING: Machine stitch and cut along the double stranded purl stitches for armhole openings (see Finishing, page 134). Graft the shoulders, and sew in the sleeves. Sew all the facings to the wrong side. Weave all loose ends into the back of the fabric. Steam lightly.

MODEL 6b

TIGHTS WITH DIAMOND DESIGN

YARN: Rauma Finullgarn. The tights shown are knit in the colors listed below.

SIZES: S (M, L)

COLORS: #443 Dark Royal–50g; #4385 Medium Blue–50g; #472 Light Blue–100g; #439 Red–200g; #458 Medium Green–50g; #455 Light Green–100g

GAUGE: 27 stitches and 32 rounds = 4 × 4 inches

NEEDLE SUGGESTION: Circular and double-point knitting needles size 2.5mm and 3mm, or size necessary to obtain gauge.

It is very important to knit to gauge otherwise the garment will be too big or too small.

TIGHTS: Using smaller double-point needles and Dark Royal, cast on 58 (62, 64) stitches for one leg. Knit in the round. Work ribbing (knit 1 through the back loop, purl 1) for 8 rounds. Change to larger needles, increase 1 stitch at the inseam, and work the pattern according to the graph. At the same time increase 2 stitches at the inseam (1 at the beginning, and 1 at the end of the round) every 5th round until you have 147 (151, 155) stitches on the needles. Knit until the leg measures 27 1/4 (28, 28 3/4) inches. Knit the other leg to match. Now bind off 14 (16, 14) stitches at the inseam of each leg. Put both legs on one circular needle with the inseams and bound-off stitches facing each other. Knit together the first and last stitch of each leg to form a center front and a center back stitch. Continue in pattern, decreasing 1 stitch on each side of the center front stitch every other round 6 times (12 stitches decreased), and decreasing 1 stitch on each side of the center back stitch every other round 10 times (20 stitches decreased). Knit even until the tights measures 37 3/4 (38 1/2, 39 1/2) inches. Using Dark Royal, knit 1 1/4 inches, purl 1 round, knit 1 1/4 inches (for casing), and bind off. Sew the casing to the purl side, and put in elastic. Sew the crotch seam. Sew all the facings to the wrong side. Weave all loose ends into the back of the fabric. Steam lightly.

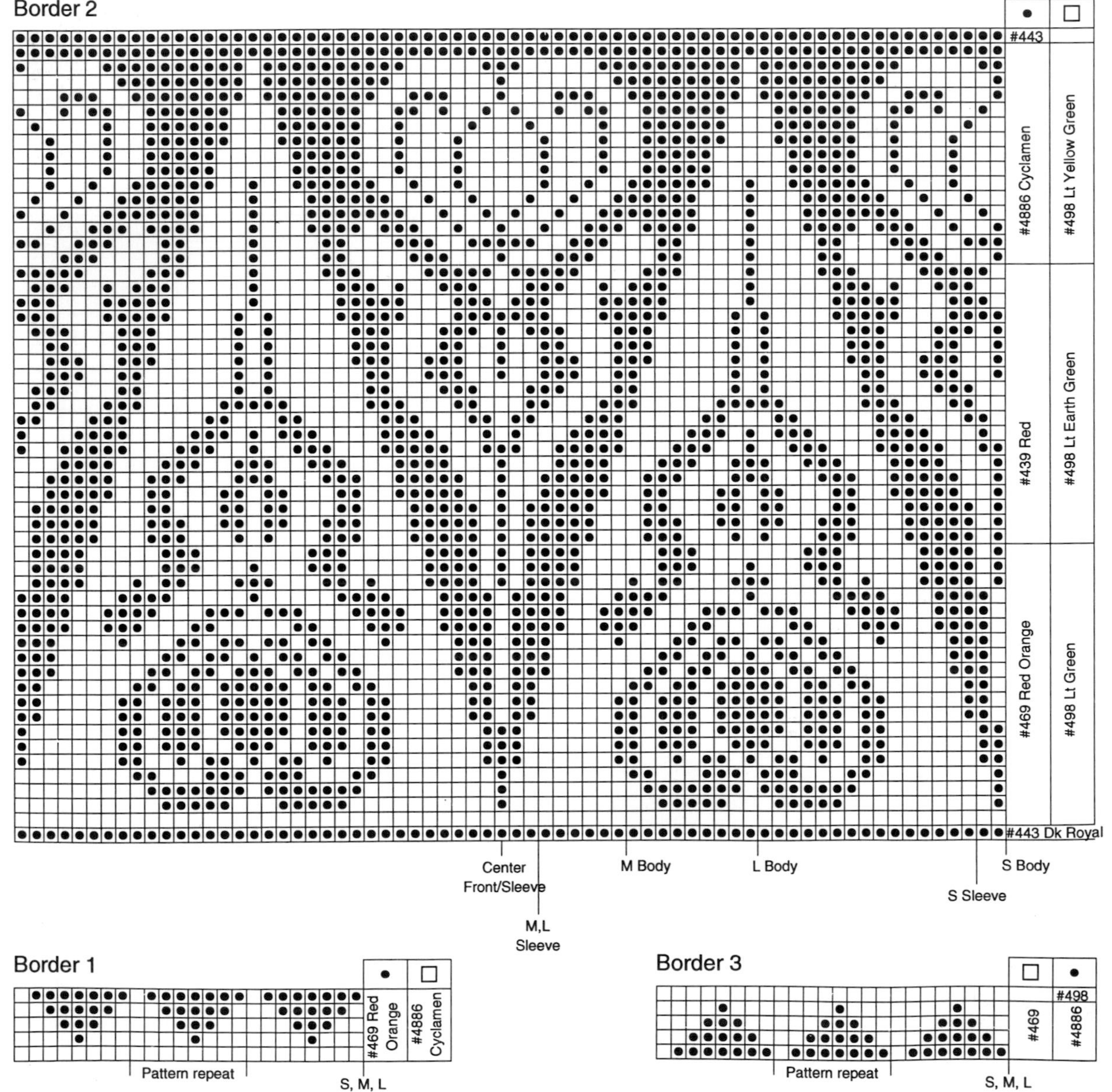

MODEL 6a

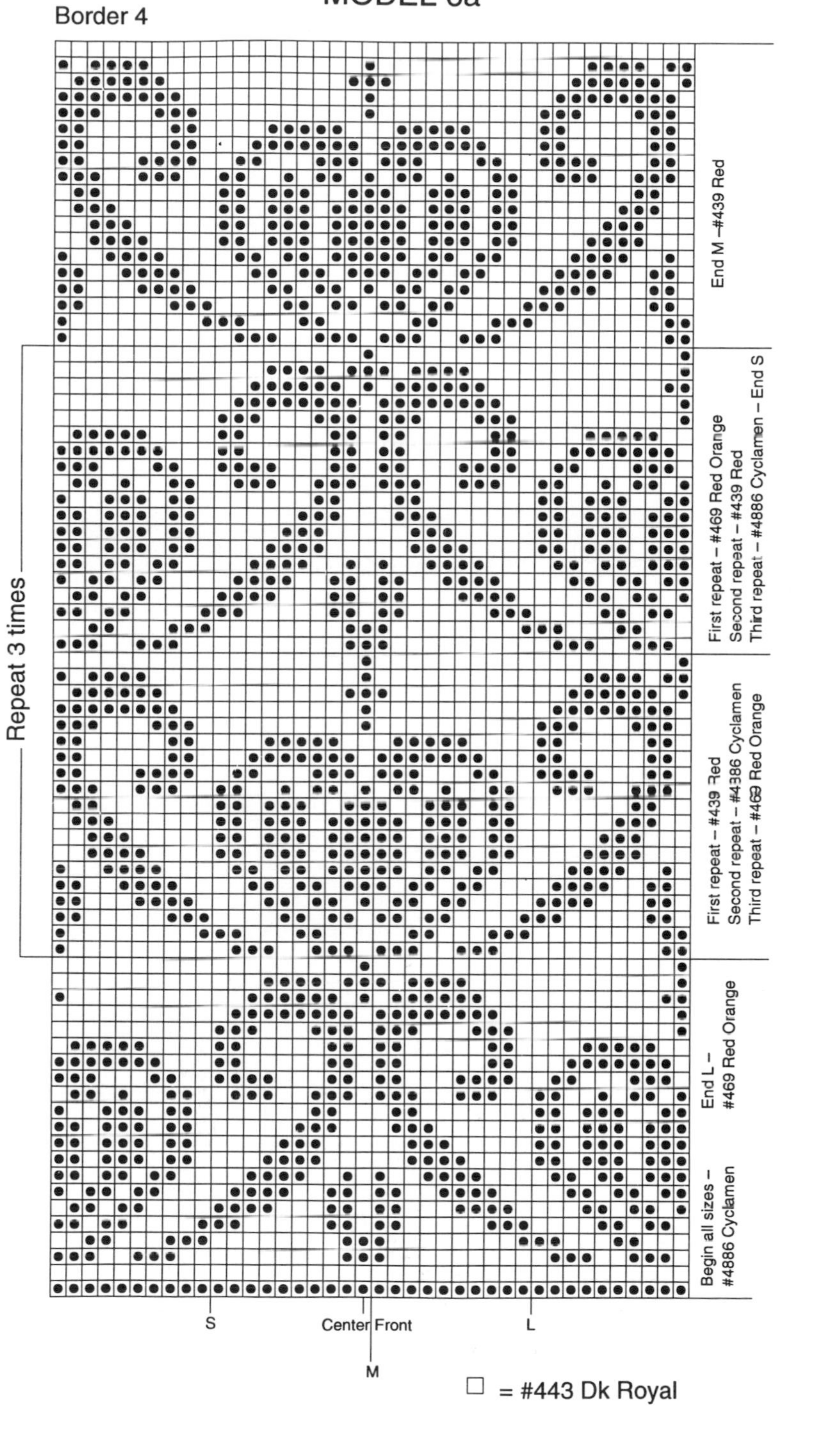

□ = #443 Dk Royal

MODEL 6b

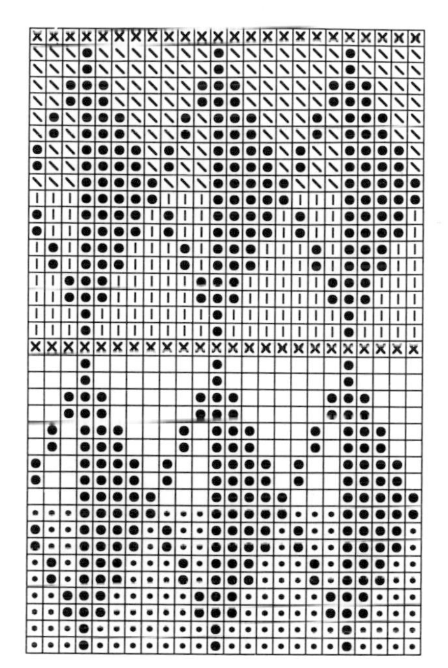

□ = #472 Lt Blue
● = #439 Red
• = #455 Lt Green
ı = #458 Med Green
× = #443 Dk Royal
⟍ = #4385 Med Blue

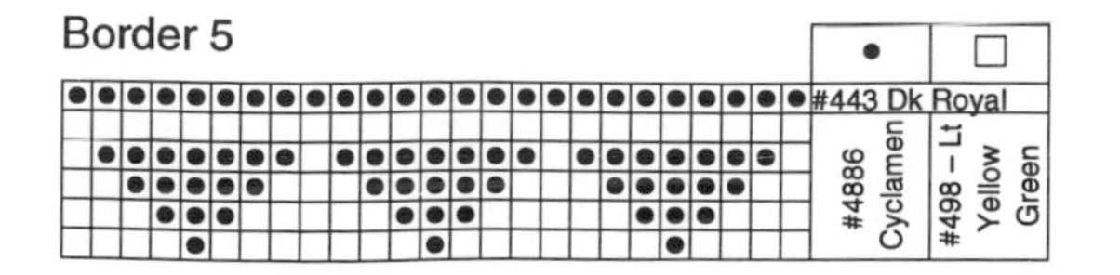

MODEL 7

SKI SWEATER WITH "WEAVE-KNIT"

In this sweater the design gradually changes up the body. A bold square design glides into a fragile star design without changing the main structure. The three related designs are not made by using the "design machine", but build on the same principle. As long as the repeats of the different designs are built on the same number of stitches, they can be easily combined. The edges of the sweater are worked in a special weave-knit technique. To produce a "woven" design on the knitted surface, the contrast yarn is carried along the knit side while the stitches are knit in the main color.

YARN: Rauma Finullgarn. The sweater shown is knit in the colors listed below.

CHARTS: pages 70–71

SIZES: S (M, L, XL, XXL)

COLORS: #464 Brown–300 (300, 350, 400, 450)g; #401 White–300 (300, 350, 400, 450)g; #458 Medium Green–50g for all sizes; #439 Red–50g for all sizes; #4886 Cyclamen–50g for all sizes; #412 Yellow–50g for all sizes

GAUGE: 27 stitches and 32 rounds = 4 × 4 inches

NEEDLE SUGGESTION: Circular and double-point knitting needles size 2.5mm and 3mm, or size necessary to obtain gauge. It is very important to knit to gauge otherwise the garment will be too big or too small.

"WEAVE-KNIT": At the same time as you knit the background color, carry the contrast color to the front or to the back of the stitches you are knitting. The design shows up as you carry the contrast yarn to the front without knitting, across the knitted background stitch when the contrast color is to form the design. Carry the contrast color to the back when the background color forms the design.

BODY: Using smaller circular needle and Brown, cast on 252 (270, 288, 306, 324) stitches. Knit in the round for 22 rounds for the hem, purl 1 round, then work Border 1 as weave-knit. Change to larger needle and increase to 256 (272, 292, 308, 324) stitches evenly spaced. In addition to Border 2, worked on the front and on the back, the sweater has stripes on each side. The stripes consist of alternating 1 stitch of Brown and 1 stitch of White. These stitches originate by increasing 1 stitch on each side of the "seam stitches". Beginning at left side seam with White, work 3 (7, 1, 5, 9) stitches in stripe pattern, knit 121 (121, 145, 145, 145) stitches of Border 2 on the front, beginning with White, work 7 (15, 1, 9, 17) stitches in stripe pattern, knit 121 (121, 145, 145, 145) stitches of Border 2 on the back, and work 4 (8, 0, 4, 8) stitches in stripe pattern. As you see on the graph, the design changes slightly. Continue to work Border 2, increasing 1 stitch in stripe pattern on each side of the seam stitches (4 stitches increased) every 6th round 7 (8, 9, 10, 11) times until you have 284 (304, 328, 348, 368) stitches total. Work until the sweater measures 12½ inches. Bind off center 9 (19, 7, 17, 27) stripe stitches at each underarm leaving 12 stitches (6 on the front, 6 on the back). On the next round, cast on 4 new stitches over the bound-off stitches. Purl those stitches using both strands on every round. They are to be machine stitched and cut later on for the sleeve openings. Work until the sweater measures 21¼ (21½, 22½, 22¾, 23½) inches. Bind off 39 (39, 39, 43, 43) stitches for the neck opening at the center front. On the next round, cast on 3 new purl stitches over the bound off stitches, and purl these stitches using both strands on every round. Continue working in the round until the garment measures 22¾ (23¼, 24, 24¾, 25½) inches. Work the same neck shaping on the back as you did for the front. Continue even until the sweater measures 24 (24¾, 25½, 26½, 26¾) inches. Bind off.

SLEEVES: Using smaller double-point needles and Brown, cast on 50 (54, 56, 56, 60) stitches. Knit in the round. Work the hem and Border 1 as for the body. Change to larger needles, and increase to 64 (68, 70, 76, 80) stitches evenly spaced. Knit the design following Border 2 as for the body. At the same time, increase 2 stitches (1 at the beginning and 1 at the end of the round) every other round until you have 156 (168, 176,

200, 210) stitches. Knit until the sleeve measures $20\frac{1}{2}$ ($20\frac{1}{2}$, $20\frac{1}{2}$, $19\frac{1}{2}$, $19\frac{1}{2}$) inches. Bind off the first stitch, and continue working the design back and forth for 1/2 ($1\frac{1}{2}$, 1, $2\frac{1}{2}$, 4) inches. With Brown, purl 1 round, knit 7 rounds to make the facing that covers the cut edge. Bind off.

FINISHING: Machine stitch and cut along the double-stranded purl stitches for armhole and neck openings (see Finishing, page 134). Graft the shoulders and sew in the sleeves. The sleeves are sewn farther in on the body than on a regular drop shoulder sweater. Using smaller needle and Brown, pick up stitches around the neck for the facing. Knit in the round, knit 1 round, purl 1 round, then knit 5 rounds increasing 1 stitch at each corner every round.

Sew all the facings to the wrong side. Weave all loose ends into the back of the fabric. Steam lightly.

HAT: Using larger needle and Brown, cast on 144 stitches. Knit in the round. Work the hem and Border 1 as for the body. Then knit Repeat D according to the graph until the hat measures 7 inches from the purl round. Thread the yarn through the stitches and gather. Sew all the facings to the wrong side. Weave all loose ends into the back of the fabric. Steam lightly. Make a small Red pompom and sew it to the top.

MODEL 7

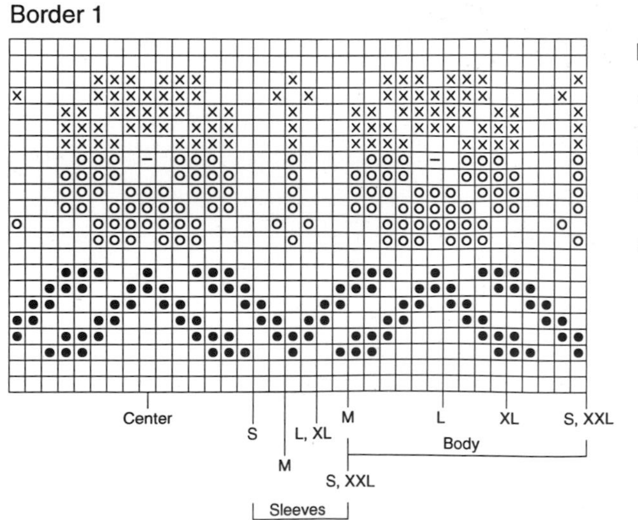

Border 2

Repeat D to end

Repeat C 1x

Repeat B 2x

Repeat A 2x

S M L XL XXL

Sleeve

S, M L, XL, XXL

Body

□ = #401 White

• = #464 Brown

RE-USING DESIGNS

Designs on a garment can have different functions. Some designs may completely cover a surface, others may decorate a collar or replace the ribbing on the lower body and sleeve edges. Consider both edge borders and all-over surface designs when you experiment with new designs.

How you choose to use your designs is as vital to your final product as how you choose to *re-use* your designs. You may choose to use all of your design variations in a single garment, or you may wish to use them selectively. It is a good exercise to explore as many different ways to use the same design as you can think of. Here, we started with a main design (A). Then we used different elements from this design to create a narrow edge or median border (B) and a surface design (C).

A

B

C

ONE STAR, TEN PATTERN BORDERS

As previously noted, a main design can be worked into several different designs. Stars have been a favorite motif in Norwegian knitting tradition throughout the years, and in other countries, the star is often used to decorate hooked rugs and beautiful embroideries. Is one star just like every other star? No, far from it. Like stars in the universe, stars used in knitting designs can be quite unique. For example, the Norwegian star, called the eight-leaf rose, can be big or small, narrow or wide, short or tall, depending on the number of stitches in each point. And even when the star is as wide as it is tall, and each point has the same number of stitches, it can still vary.

A. This is the shape of the star we will begin with. It has been placed on striped and checkered surfaces.

B. The star has a square in the middle and at each corner, and is on a checkered background. The small checks give a variegated impression compared to the larger black-and-white checkered areas. We actually see three shades using only two colors.

C. Large white squares at the corners of the star and an *X* in the middle make the star look smaller. Two points from the star create the design element for a zigzag border, framing the star at the top and at the bottom. The square from the middle of the star is made into a square design in the lower part of the graph, which could be used as an allover surface design. In this case, the individual stars are only meant to function as borders.

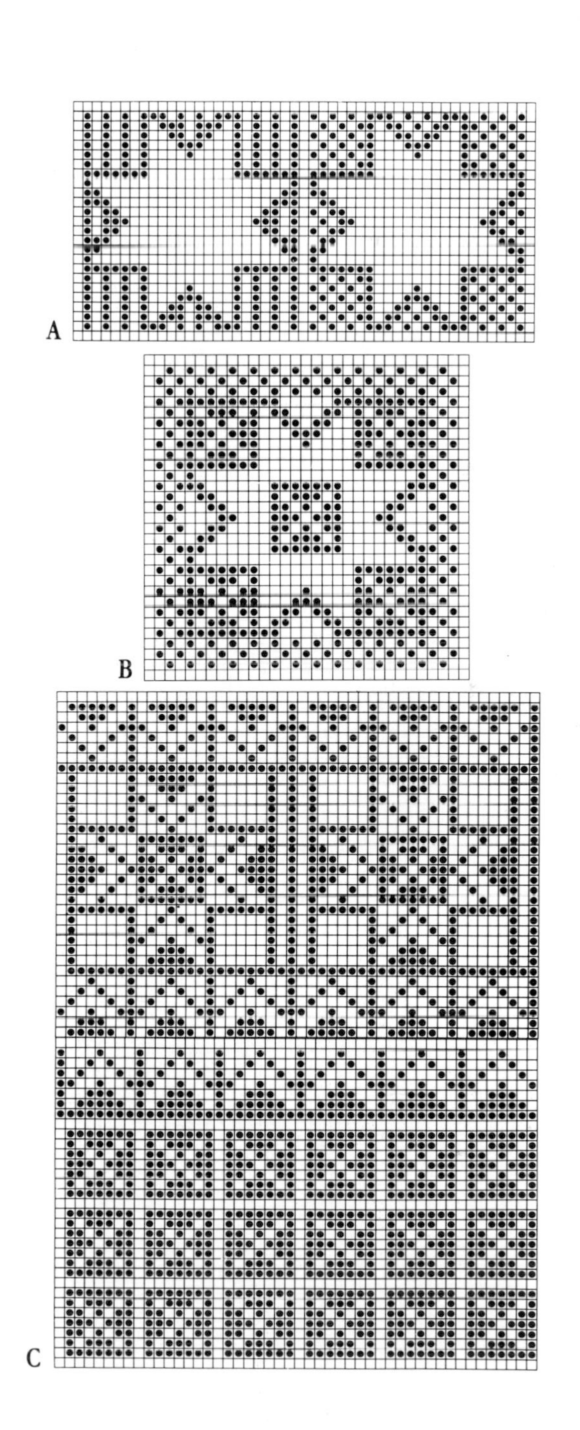

In Model 9, you'll find the original star shape with a circular design in the middle of it. Because the stars are not placed right on top of each other, the design does not seem too tight. The striped background ensures that the design does not become too busy.

D. Here, the original star shape is used in a positive-negative design. The stars alternate between a light and a dark main color. Narrow light diagonal stripes tie them together to a net of hexagons, creating a well-integrated design.

E. The black stars in D have been fitted into a checkerboard design of squares with Xs.

F. This time the white stars have been fitted into the checkerboard design. As you can see, the effect is quite different.

D

E

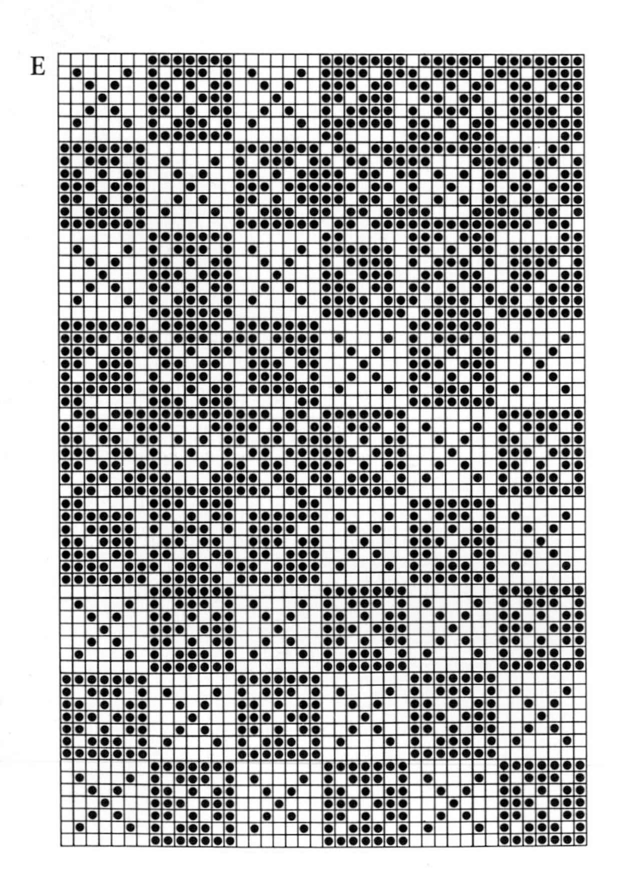

F

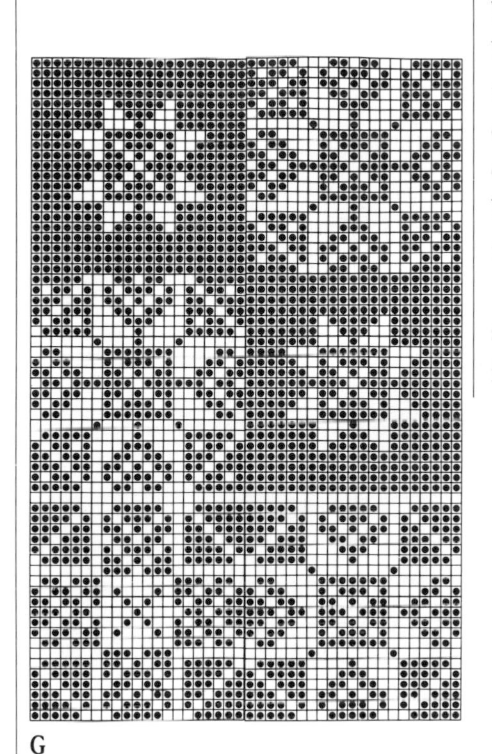

G

G. A black and a white star create a border at the bottom of this design. The black star (to the left) is almost lost against the background, while the white star is seen quite clearly. Above the border is a surface design where every second star is filled with black squares so that it seems much smaller than the original star.

H. The same number of design elements surround these stars on all sides. The square in the middle of each star has been expanded, so that the star now looks like an octagon-shaped flower.

I. The motif in the middle of the star has been varied even further, creating a new "flower". The stars are placed on a mixed background which is broken up by a small checkered design between the stars.

J. The middle of the stars have changed somewhat, and they lay on top of a checkered background.

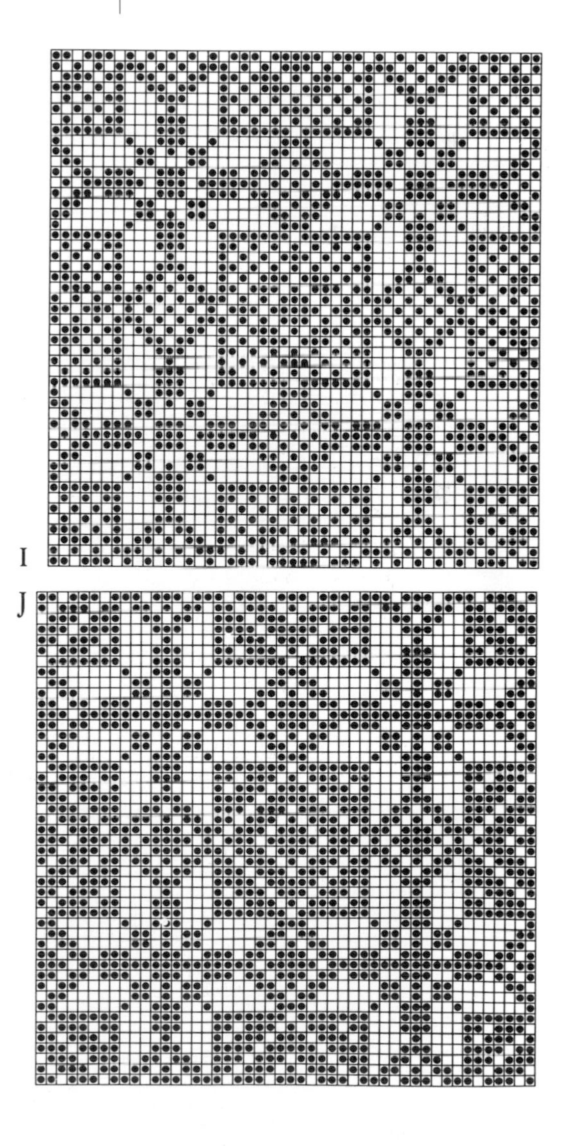

I

J

H

a
b
d

Star shapes in color

a. Natural shades of wool were combined with blue for this star. Blue and natural colors blend well together, just as bare rock and blue sky blend in nature. The brown and beige colors enhance the blue, making it more beautiful and shiny.

b. These colors looked good together as balls of yarns next to each other, but they lost some pizazz when they were combined in a design. This is probably because approximately the same amount of each color was used in the design.

c. In this swatch, we used one shade of blue and several shades of beige. In this case, the natural colors turned out to be a dead end street. A sweater in these colors would be depressing to knit and to wear.

d. The soft tones were replaced with strong colors and a shiny cotton yarn (Rauma Kvartett). It is amazing how the change of color brought out the design in a completely new way. The zigzag border was dropped, and the stripes between the rows of stars were knitted in much stronger colors than the stars themselves. The resulting horizontal stripes changed the whole impression of the design.

In the three swatches, the same design changed character through the use of different colors. The design itself was always worked in a single color, but the main color was varied. The main color appeared different against the compact striped background than against the open stars. Against the stripes, the main color blended with the dark contrast color; against the stars, it showed up quite clearly. In all three of these examples there is a striking contrast between the main colors. This effect is possible when the contrast color is the darkest color.

MODEL 8

MAN'S CARDIGAN WITH STARS AND SQUARES

The eye perceives round and triangular forms as being more dynamic than square forms. The motifs framed by squares in this cardigan appear calm. The colors also contribute to the calmness of the garment. Notice how the colors are distributed. Every row of squares is knitted in charcoal plus another color, while the stars are knitted in a variation of several colors. Even though only two colors are worked at a time, the cardigan gives a rich and colorful impression. At first glance, it looks as if the cardigan is knitted with four colors. But there are actually two shades of blue. This makes for a more active blend of colors.

YARN: Rauma Finullgarn. The sweater shown is knit in the colors listed below.

ACCESSORIES: 7 pewter clasps

CHART: page 80

SIZES: L (XL, XXL)

COLORS: #4387 Dark Charcoal–300 (350, 400)g; #4385 Medium Blue–100 (100, 150)g; #471 Light Violet–50 (50, 100)g; #451 Grey Blue–100 (100, 150)g; #4287 Light Grey–50 (50, 100)g

GAUGE: 27 stitches and 32 rounds = 4 × 4 inches

NEEDLE SUGGESTION: Circular and double-point knitting needles size 2.5mm and 3mm or size necessary to obtain gauge. It is very important to knit to gauge otherwise the garment will be too big or too small.

BODY: Using smaller circular needle and Dark Charcoal, cast on 275 (303, 331) stitches. Knit in the round for 8 rounds for the hem, purl 1 round, then knit 8 rounds. Change to larger needle and Border 1 according to the graph. The round starts at the left side: Knit 7 (14, 21) stitches of the square design, then 1 stitch Dark Charcoal (a 1-stitch vertical stripe), the Front Star design, 1 stitch Dark Charcoal (a 1-stitch vertical stripe), purl 3 stitches using both strands to be machine stitched and cut open for the front opening, 1 stitch Dark Charcoal (a 1-stitch vertical stripe), the Front Star design, 1 stitch Dark Charcoal (a 1-stitch vertical stripe), and 7 (14, 21) stitches of the square design. You are now at the right side of the cardigan. Knit the squares on the sides so that they alternate between light and dark. Knit the back as follows: 7 (14, 21) stitches of the square design, 1 stitch Dark Charcoal (a 1-stitch vertical stripe), 3 repeats of the Back Star design, 1 stitch Dark Charcoal (a 1-stitch vertical stripe), and 7 (14, 21) stitches of the square design. The cardigan has increases on the sides. Continue in pattern, and at the same time increase 2 stitches at each side "seam" every 4th round until you have total 327 (355, 383) stitches. Then knit even until the cardigan measures $22\frac{1}{2}$ ($22\frac{3}{4}$, $23\frac{1}{4}$) inches. Bind off the center front 43 stitches for the front neck. On the next round, cast on 4 new stitches over the bound off stitches. Purl these 4 stitches using both strands on every round. They are to be machine stitched and cut open for the neck opening. Continue knitting even until the garment measures $24\frac{3}{4}$ ($25\frac{1}{2}$, $26\frac{1}{2}$) inches. Now shape the back neck by binding off the center back 40 stitches. On the next round, cast on 4 new stitches over the bound-off stitches and purl these stitches as you did for the front neck. Continue until the cardigan measures approximately $25\frac{1}{2}$ ($26\frac{1}{2}$, $26\frac{3}{4}$) inches. Finish with a complete square. Bind off.

SLEEVES: Using smaller double-point needles and Dark Charcoal, cast on 56 (56, 60) stitches. Knit in the round. Work the lower edge as you did the body. Change to larger needles and increase to 76 (70, 80) stitches evenly spaced. Begin Border 2 as marked on the graph knitting the last "seam stitch" in Dark Charcoal. Upon completion of Border 2, continue with the center star of the Front Star pattern of Border 1. At the same time, increase 1 stitch on each side of the seam stitch every other round until you have 176 (200, 210) stitches total. Knit until the sleeve measures 20 ($19\frac{1}{2}$, $19\frac{1}{2}$) inches. To make the facing that covers up the cut edge, purl 1 round, knit 7 rounds. Bind off.

FINISHING: Machine stitch and cut along the double-stranded purl stitches for armhole and neck openings (see Finishing, page 134). Graft the shoulders and sew in the sleeves. Using Dark Charcoal, pick up stitches along the front edges and around the neck. Work the facing as follows: Knit 1 row on the knit side, knit 1 row on the purl side, then work stockinette stitch for 7 rows increasing 1 stitch every row at the corners of the neck opening, and decrease 1 stitch every row at the upper edge of each front band. Bind off. Sew all the facings to the wrong side. Weave all loose ends into the back of the fabric. Steam lightly. Sew clasps along the front.

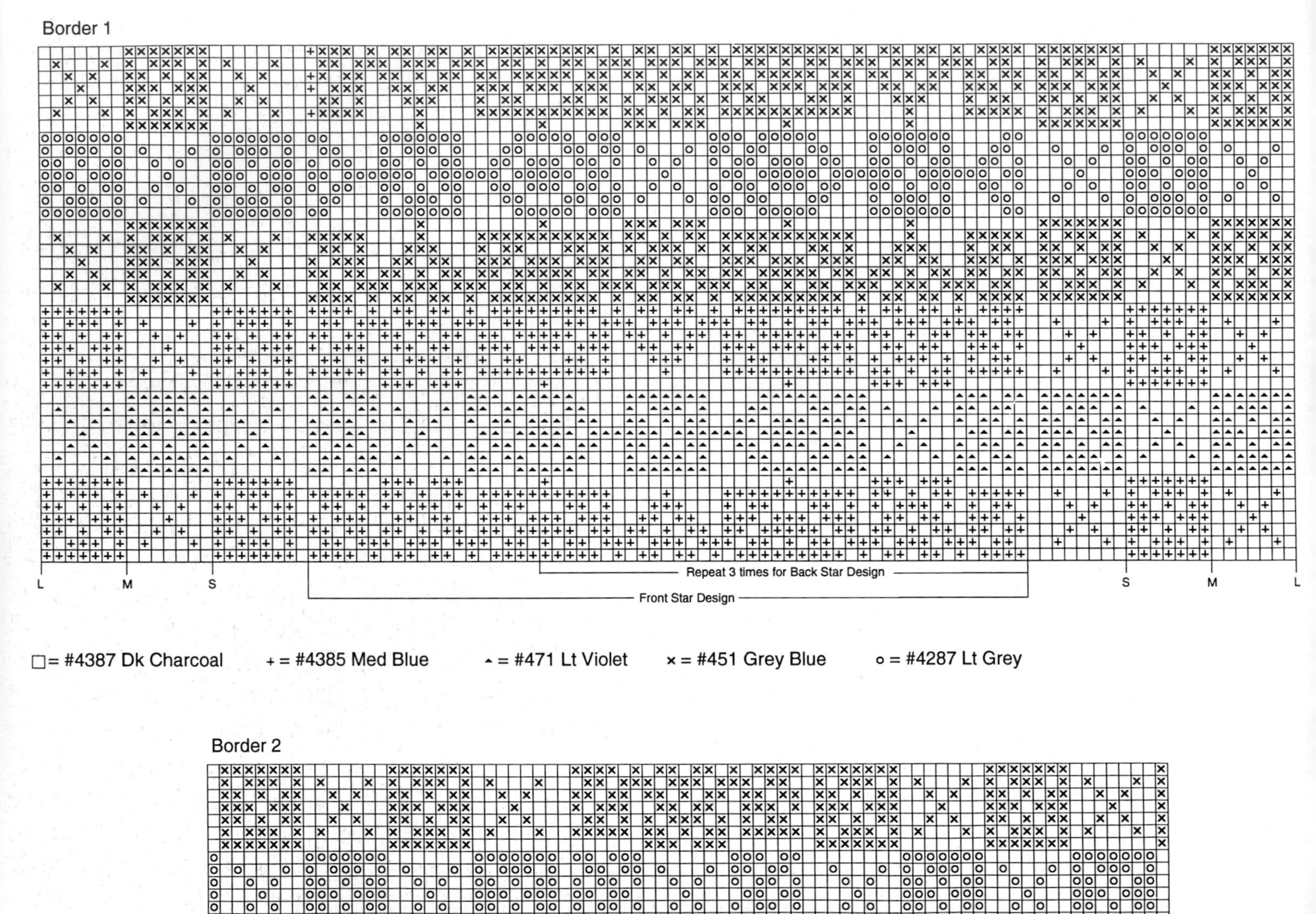

MODEL 9

PULLOVER WITH STARS AND COLOR VARIATION

This sweater is covered with stars. Notice how the main color keeps changing. At the shoulder it is yellow, while the rest of the sweater it is rose colored. Without changing the design at all, the sweater has a yoke that differs from the rest of the design.

YARN: Rauma Finullgarn. The sweater shown is knit in the colors listed below.

CHART: page 82

SIZES: S (M, L)

COLORS: #410 Dark Brown–250 (300, 300)g; #440 Wooden Rose–150g for each size; #490 Dusky Rose–100g for each size; #4087 Light Rose–100g for each size; #444 Deep Rust–50g for each size; #434 Light Rust–50g for each size; #450 Yellow Gold–50g for each size; #439 Red–50g for each size

GAUGE: 27 stitches and 32 rounds = 4 × 4 inches

NEEDLE SUGGESTION: Circular and double-point knitting needles size 2.5mm and 3mm, or size necessary to obtain gauge. It is very important to knit to gauge otherwise the garment will be too big or too small.

BODY: Using smaller circular needle and Light Rust, cast on 264 (288, 312) stitches. Knit in the round for 8 rounds for the hem, purl 1 round, knit 8 rounds. Change to larger needle and Dark Brown, and increase to 292 (316, 340) stitches evenly spaced. Knit stripes alternating 1 Dark Brown, and 1 Yellow Gold for 7 rounds. Begin working according to the graph: Knit 6 star borders according to color direction 1, and 1 star border according to color direction 2. When the pullover measures 21¼ (21½, 21¾) inches, shape for the front neck by binding off the 39 center front stitches. Then work back and forth until the garment measures 23¼ inches. To shape the back neck, bind off in the same way as you did for the front neck. Work until the pullover measures 24½ (24½, 24¾) inches. After finishing the last star border, work stripes alternating 1 Red and 1 Dark Brown until desired length. Bind off.

SLEEVES: Using smaller double-point needles and Red, cast on 50 (54, 56) stitches. Knit in the round for 4 rounds for the hem, purl 1 round, and knit 4 rounds. Change to larger needles and Dark Brown, and increase to 64 (68, 76) stitches evenly spaced. Knit stripes alternating 1 Dark Brown, and 1 Yellow Gold for 5 rounds. Work the graph following color direction 1. At the same time, increase 2 stitches (1 stitch at the beginning and 1 stitch at the end of the round) every 3rd round until you have 156 (168, 176) stitches. After the 6th star border, knit stripes alternating 1 Dark Brown, and 1 Yellow Gold until the sleeve measures 20½ (20½, 20) inches. To make the facing that covers up the cut edge, purl 1 round, knit 7 rounds. Bind off.

FINISHING: Machine stitch and cut along the double-stranded purl stitches for armhole openings (see Finishing, page 134). Using Red, pick up stitches around the neck. Join to a round, and knit 4 rounds decreasing 1 stitch at each corner every round. Purl 1 round, then knit 4 rounds increasing 1 stitch at each corner every round. Bind off. Sew all the facings to the wrong side. Weave all loose ends into the back of the fabric. Steam lightly.

HAT: Using larger circular needle and Red, cast on 144 stitches. Knit in the round for 1¼ inches, purl 1 round, knit 4 rounds. Knit one star border according to color direction 2. Change to Dark Brown, purl 1 round, then decrease as follows:

Knit 2 together, knit 6, repeat between *'s around.

Knit 6 rounds.

Next round: *Knit 2 together, knit 5*, repeat between *'s around.

Knit 5 rounds.

Next round: *Knit 2 together, knit 4*, repeat between *'s around.

Knit 4 rounds.

Next round: *Knit 2 together, knit 3*, repeat between *'s around.

Knit 3 rounds.

Next round: *Knit 2 together, knit 2*, repeat between *'s around.

Knit 2 rounds.

Next round: *Knit 2 together, knit 1*, repeat between *'s around.

Knit 1 round.

Next round: Knit 2 together around. Put the remaining stitches on

yarn and gather. Sew the hem to the wrong side. Weave all loose ends into the back of the fabric. Steam lightly.

MODEL 9

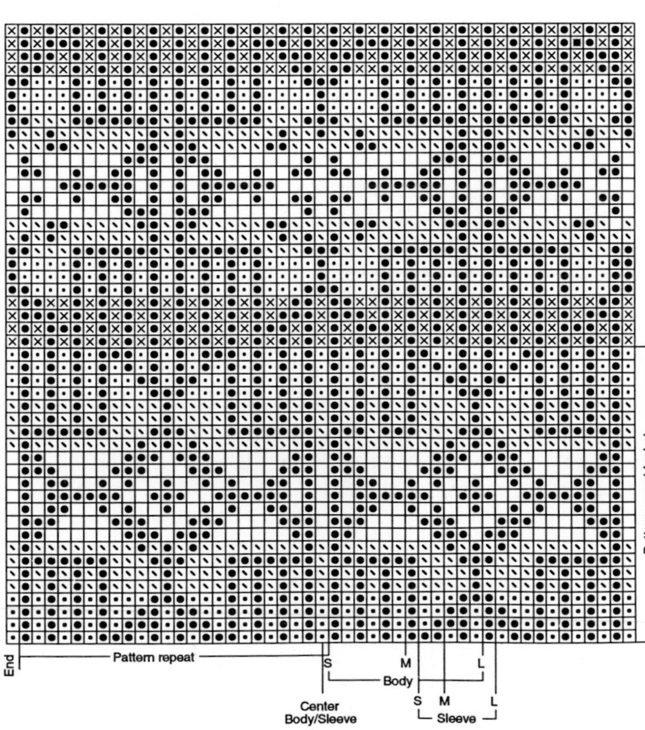

STAR COLOR 1

- • = #410 Dk Brown
- · = #440 Wooden Rose
- ˎ = #490 Dusky Rose
- × = #444 Deep Rust
- □ = #4087 Lt Rose

STAR COLOR 2

- • = #410 Dk Brown
- · = #440 Wooden Rose
- ˎ = #434 Lt Rust
- × = ##439 Red
- □ = #450 Med Gold

PART III
GIVING SHAPE TO A GARMENT

PLACING DESIGNS ON A GARMENT

In Norwegian and Nordic knitting tradition, there are certain "rules" as to how and where different designs should be placed on a garment. These "rules" have stayed with us for so long, that it is sometimes difficult to think in new ways.

A sweater with sewn-in sleeves often has a border above the ribbing on the body, a smaller design in the middle of the body, and a larger design on the yoke. In addition, it may have a border at the bottom or at the top of the sleeves.

A raglan sweater often has a design on the yoke, and sometimes a design above the ribbing. On a hat, a design is usually placed at the bottom, on the cuff, or along the ribbing.

There is nothing wrong with these kinds of design distributions. In fact, there are probably many practical and aesthetic reasons for this tradition. Besides, these designs are often exceptionally beautiful, which is why they've been around so long. However, if you are able to break from tradition, you'll discover many other unique design variations. Using the elements of the same basic designs, you can make garments that are quite different from each other. As mentioned previously, it is well worth your time to figure out the possibilities, first with sketches on a piece of paper, and then on garments.

Following are seven sketches showing different ways of placing designs on a sweater. Have a look, and see if you can discover any other designs. Think of ways that these designs could go on a sweater with sewn-in sleeves. Make five sketches of sweaters laying flat, choose some borders from your own folder, and try different placements. You do not have to be concerned with the final product at this point—this is an exercise to aid in planning a garment.

Make three copies of each sketch, find your crayons or markers, and make three color suggestions for each sweater. This exercise can also be used to design hats, skirts, mittens, and pants.

1. Start with a design based on squares. By alternating between positive and negative features such as light and dark or two contrast colors, you can create a diamond-like design covering all of the body, a centered design to tighten up the look, or a frame around the body

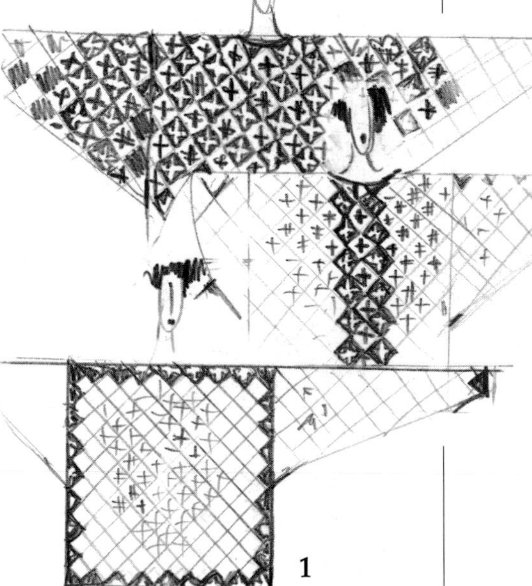

1

2. This design is based on stripes and zigzag borders.

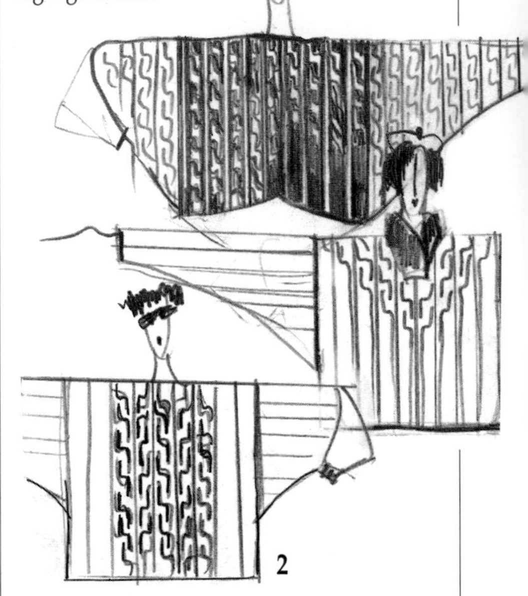

2

Positive-negative design elements can be used to make the body look heavy and the sleeves light. You can achieve a more sophisticated look by combining two designs. In this case, the zigzag glides over onto the stripes, creating a zigzag designed-yoke, while the rest of the sweater is striped. The zigzag can also be kept strictly as the center of the design, while the rest of the sweater is striped.

3. Different designs can be combined to create an asymmetrical or symmetrical look.

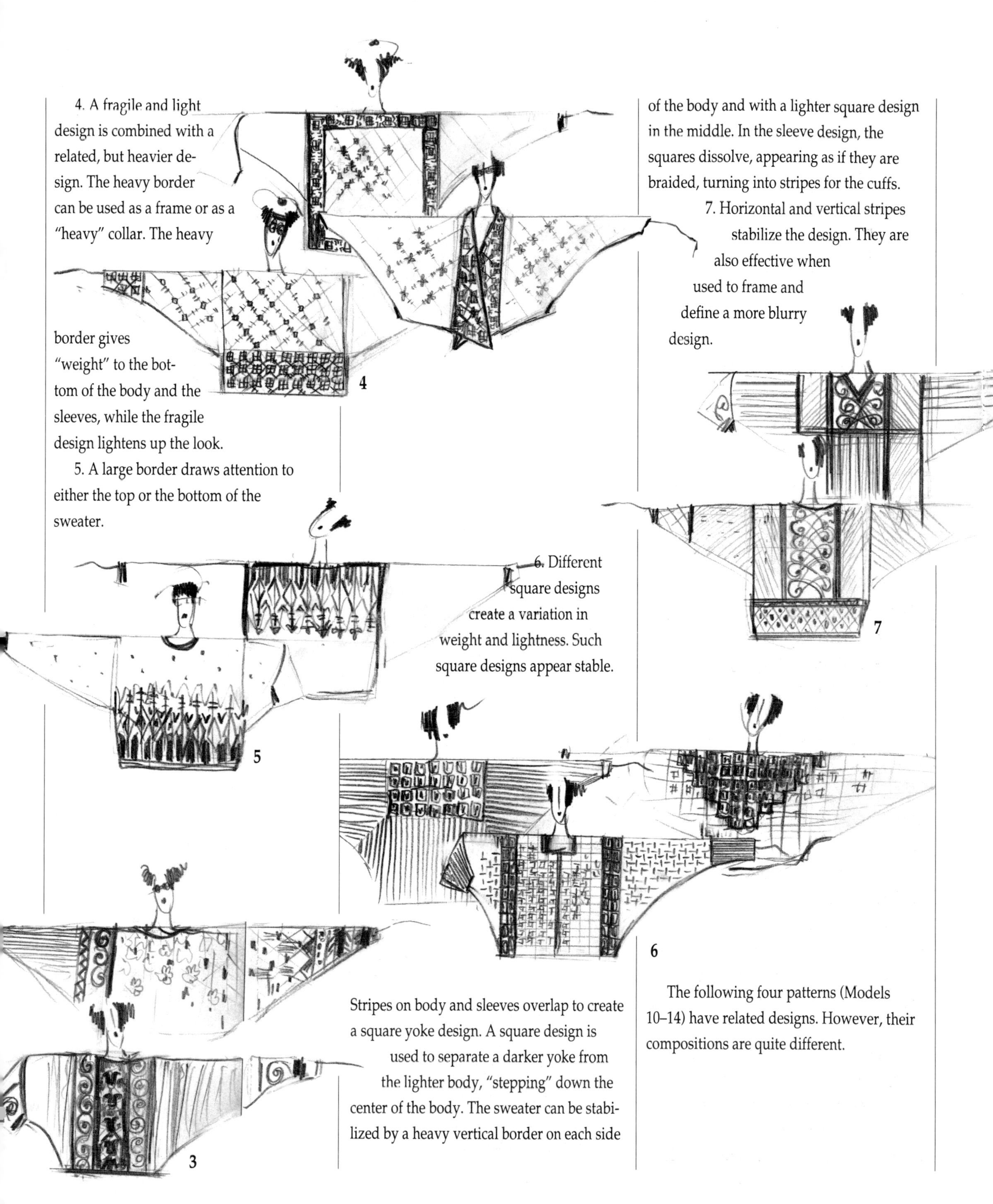

4. A fragile and light design is combined with a related, but heavier design. The heavy border can be used as a frame or as a "heavy" collar. The heavy border gives "weight" to the bottom of the body and the sleeves, while the fragile design lightens up the look.

5. A large border draws attention to either the top or the bottom of the sweater.

6. Different square designs create a variation in weight and lightness. Such square designs appear stable.

Stripes on body and sleeves overlap to create a square yoke design. A square design is used to separate a darker yoke from the lighter body, "stepping" down the center of the body. The sweater can be stabilized by a heavy vertical border on each side of the body and with a lighter square design in the middle. In the sleeve design, the squares dissolve, appearing as if they are braided, turning into stripes for the cuffs.

7. Horizontal and vertical stripes stabilize the design. They are also effective when used to frame and define a more blurry design.

The following four patterns (Models 10–14) have related designs. However, their compositions are quite different.

MODEL 10

PULLOVER WITH ROSES KNIT FROM WRIST TO WRIST

This sweater is knitted from sleeve to sleeve, and therefore has no traditional sleeve and body. It is knitted as a cylinder, expanding and closing in again. After it is knit, it is cut open at the top and the bottom.

To mark the "body", the middle section has a darker main color and a design different from the "sleeves". The rose and turquoise are bright against the charcoal and dark blue. The idea is to create a look that will remind one of stained-glass paintings.

YARN: Rauma Finullgarn. The sweater knit is shown in the colors listed below.

CHARTS: page 88–89

SIZES: S (M, L)

COLORS: #467 Midnight Blue–150g; #4387 Dark Charcoal–100g; #482 Dark Blue–50g; #437 Blue–100g; #4887 Sage Green–50g; #4186 Sea Green–50g; #483 Turquoise–50g; #451 Grey Blue–50g; #4385 Medium Blue–50g; #478 Medium Rose–50g; #456 Bright Rose–50g; #439 Red–50g.

GAUGE: 27 stitches and 32 rounds = 4 × 4 inches.

NEEDLE SUGGESTION: Circular and double-point knitting needles size 3mm, or size necessary to obtain gauge. It is very important to knit to gauge otherwise the garment will be too big or too small.

PULLOVER: Using double-point needles and Blue, cast on 57 stitches. Knit in the round for 1 1/2 inches for the hem, purl 1 round, knit 3 rounds. Now start working the graph. Knit Borders 1, 2, 3, and 4 with the color changes specified in the graph. At the same time, increase 2 stitches (1 stitch at the beginning and 1 stitch at the end of the round) every 4th round until you have 79 (81, 83) stitches. Now increase 2 stitches every round. You can change to a short circular needle when you have enough stitches to reach comfortably around the needle. After more increases, you need to change to a longer needle. Repeat Border 4 with the specified color changes and continue to increase 2 stitches every round until you have a total of 243 (245, 247) stitches. Knit until the sleeve measures 19 1/4 (19 1/2, 20) inches. You have now finished the first sleeve.

To avoid knitting back and forth on the body, cast on 3 new stitches at the beginning of the round. Purl these 3 stitches using both colors of each round; they will later be machine stitched and cut open. Work Border 2, then five repeats of the flowers in Border 5 with the color changes specified in the graph. The center of the 3rd repeat will be the front and back center of the pullover. The remaining half of the sweater is a mirror image of what you have knit thus far, and you will decrease where you earlier increased. Finish Border 5 and then work Border 2. Bind off the three purl stitches. Before you continue knitting, machine stitch and cut along the double-stranded purl stitches for the lower opening (see Finishing, page 134). (You can also wait until you have finished all the knitting, but it will be harder to do the machine sewing at that point).

Knit Border 4 to match the first sleeve and begin working decreases where you finished working increases on the other sleeve. Decrease 2 stitches (1 at the beginning and 1 at the end of the round) every round until you have 79 (81, 83) stitches left. Knit the Borders as for the first sleeve, and decrease 2 stitches (1 at the beginning and 1 at the end of the round) every 4th round until you have 56 stitches left. Make the hem like the other sleeve.

FINISHING: If you have not already done it, machine stitch and cut the lower opening. Mark, machine stitch, and cut the boat neck opening. The neck opening is 11 3/4 inches wide. Using Blue, pick up stitches around the lower edge and knit in the round for 1 round, purl 1 round, then knit 8 rounds for the hem increasing 2 stitches on each side every round. Bind off and sew the hem to the purl side. Pick up stitches around the neck for the facing. Knit the hem as for the body, increasing 2 stitches on each side of the neck every round to make the facing lay flat. Sew all the facings to the wrong side. Weave all loose ends into the back of the fabric. Steam lightly.

HAT: Using Blue, cast on 144 stitches. Knit in the round for 1¼ inches for the hem, purl 1 round, knit 3 rounds. Knit Border 1 as for the sleeve. Change to Midnight Blue. Knit 3 rounds, purl 1 round, and decrease as follows:

Knit 2 together, knit 6, repeat between *'s around. Knit 6 rounds.

Next round: *Knit 2 together, knit 5*, repeat between *'s around.

Knit 5 rounds.

Next round: *Knit 2 together, knit 4*, repeat between *'s around.

Knit 4 rounds.

Next round: *Knit 2 together, knit 3*, repeat between *'s around.

Knit 3 rounds.

Next round: *Knit 2 together, knit 2*, repeat between *'s around. Knit 2 rounds.

Next round: *Knit 2 together, knit 1*, repeat between *'s around. Knit 1 round.

Last round: Knit 2 together around. Pull the yarn through the remaining stitches and gather. Sew all the facings to the wrong side. Weave all loose ends into the back of the fabric. Steam lightly.

MODEL 10

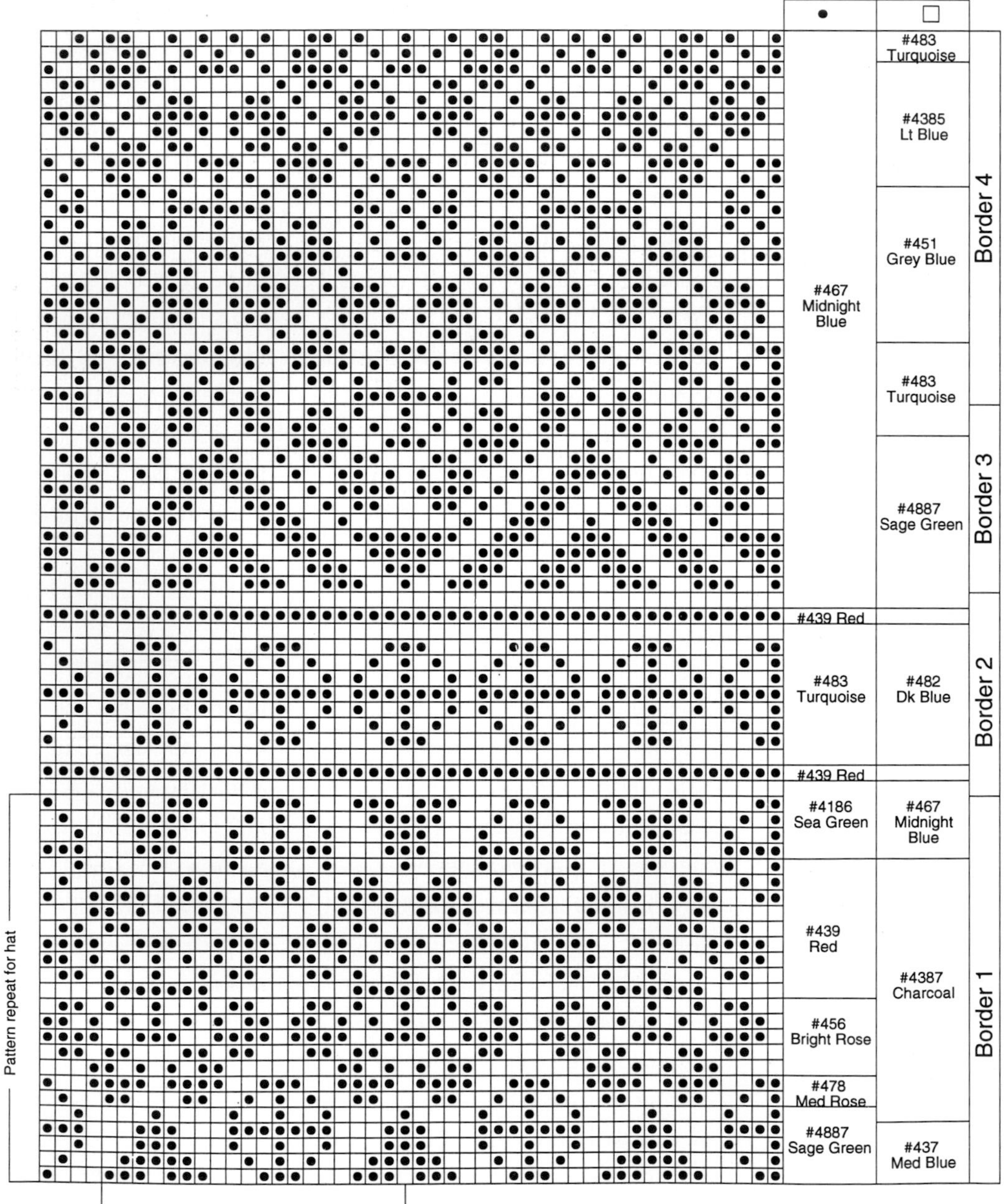

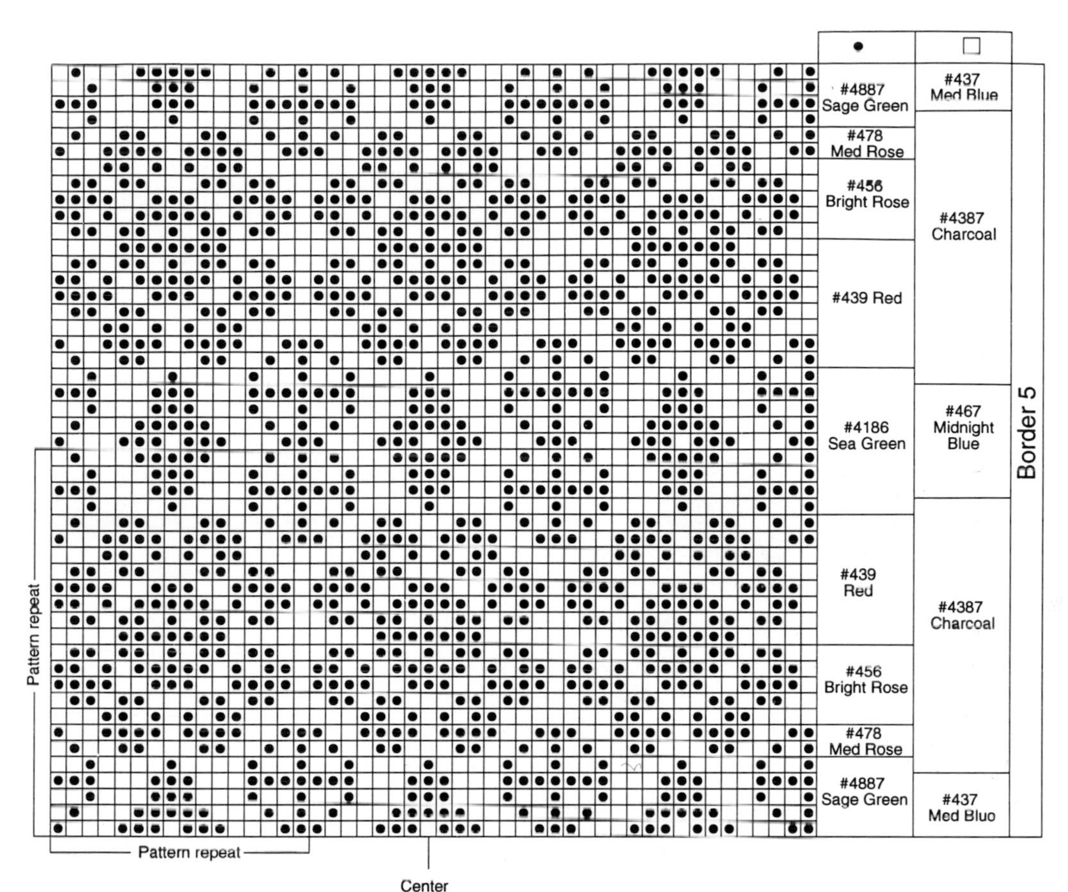
•
□
#4887
Sage Green
#437
Med Blue
#478
Med Rose
#456
Bright Rose
#4387
Charcoal
#439 Red
#4186
Sea Green
#467
Midnight
Blue
Border 5
#439
Red
#4387
Charcoal
#456
Bright Rose
#478
Med Rose
#4887
Sage Green
#437
Med Bluo
Pattern repeat
Pattern repeat
Center
Shoulder/Sleeve

MODEL 11

CHILD'S CARDIGAN WITH A SHAWL COLLAR

MODEL 12

PULLOVER WITH FLOWERS

The child's cardigan is calmer and "fuller" in its color expression than the previous garment. Stars in pink and purple lay on a dark, charcoal background. This creates a controlled contrast to the collar, which swarms with colors. Simple, narrow stripes finish off the collar and the sleeves.

The pullover is even more simple. There is nothing but the flower design on the dark background, and it is all pulled together by the color along the edges.

YARN: Rauma Finullgarn. The sweater shown is knit in the colors listed below.

CHARTS: page 93

SIZES: 9 years (12 years)

COLORS: #4387 Dark Charcoal–250 (300)g; #4887 Sage Green–100 (150)g; #456 Bright Rose–50g; #439 Red–50g; #479 Light Pink–50g; #467 Midnight Blue–50g; #4385 Medium Blue–50g; #471 Light Violet–50g; #496 Red Violet–50g.

GAUGE: 27 stitches and 32 rounds = 4 × 4 inches

NEEDLE SUGGESTION: Circular and double-point knitting needles size 2.5mm and 3mm, or size necessary to obtain gauge. It is very important to knit to gauge otherwise the garment will be too big or too small.

BODY: Using smaller circular needle and Medium Blue, cast on 181 (203) stitches. Purl the 4 center front stitches using both strands on all rounds; they are to be machine stitched and cut open later on. Knit 7 rounds for the hem, purl 1 round, knit 5 rounds. Change to larger needle, and knit vertical stripes alternating 1 stitch Dark Charcoal and 1 stitch Sage Green for 10 rounds. Using Dark Charcoal, knit 3 rounds, then Border 1 according to the graph. Work until the garment measures 18 ½ (20 ½) inches. Then shape for the back neck (there is no front neck shaping) as follows: Bind off 23 (45) stitches at the center back. On the next round, cast on 4 new stitches over the bound-off stitches. Purl these 4 stitches using both strands on every round. Continue working in the round and decrease 1 stitch on each side of the back neck every round 12 times. Continue in pattern until the cardigan measures 20 (22) inches. Knit the next round using Dark Charcoal as follows: knit 32 stitches, bind off 3 stitches to mark placement of the sleeve opening, knit 32 stitches, bind off the 4 purl stitches at the back neck, knit 32 stitches, bind off 3 stitches to mark placement of the other sleeve opening, knit 32 stitches, and bind off the 4 purl stitches at the center front. Place stitches on holders.

SLEEVES: Using smaller double-point needles and Medium Blue, cast on 36 (40) stitches. Knit in the round. Knit the hem as for the body. Change to larger needles and knit the vertical stripes alternating 1 stitch Charcoal and 1 stitch Turquoise. The first stitch on the round is a "seam stitch" and is knitted in Charcoal all the time. Increase 1 stitch on each side of the seam stitch every 3rd round until you have 44 (44) stitches. Knit stripes for 10 rounds. Using Dark Charcoal, knit 3 rounds, increasing to 60 (64) stitches evenly spaced on the third round, then Border 1 increasing 2 stitches (one on each side of the seam stitch) every other round until you have 122 (136) stitches. Knit until the sleeve measures 13 ¾ (15 ¾) inches. To make the facing that covers up the cut edge, purl 1 round, knit 7 rounds. Bind off.

FINISHING: Machine stitch and cut along the double-stranded purl stitches for the front opening (see Finishing, page 134).

Mark, stitch, and cut the sleeve openings (see Finishing, page 134). Graft the shoulders and sew in the sleeves.

COLLAR: Using Dark Charcoal, pick up 305 (353) stitches as follows: 136 (152) the stitches along each front, 32 (48) stitches across the back neck, and 1 stitch to balance the pattern. When picking up stitches along the front edges, pick up 2 to 3 stitches along the front edges of the hem (below the purl round). Cast on 4 extra stitches before knitting in the round. These 4 stitches are to be purled using a double strand on every round, and will be machine stitched and cut open later on. Using Dark Charcoal, knit 3 rounds, then work Border 2 according to the graph. Knit vertical stripes alternating 1 stitch Dark Charcoal and 1 stitch Sage Green for 3 rounds. Using Dark Charcoal, purl 1 round, then work the vertical stripes again until the facing (the back side of the collar) is 1 round wider than the front side. Bind off. Machine stitch and cut along the double-stranded purl stitches for lower edge of collar opening (see Finishing, page 134). Sew the collar at the lower edges from the purl side. Sew all the facings to the wrong side. Weave all loose ends into the back of the fabric. Steam lightly.

PULLOVER WITH FLOWERS

YARN: Rauma Finullgarn. The sweater shown is knit in the colors listed below.

SIZES: 6 yrs (9 yrs, 12 yrs, S, M, L, XL, XXL)

COLORS: #4387 Dark Charcoal–200 (250, 250, 300, 350, 400, 450, 500)g; #4088 Medium Violet–100g for all sizes; #4887 Sage Green–50g; #471 Light Violet–50g; #479 Light Pink–50g; #439 Red–50g; #456 Bright Rose–50g.

GAUGE: 27 stitches and 32 rounds = 4 × 4 inches

NEEDLE SUGGESTION: Circular and double-point knitting needles size 2.5mm and 3mm, or size necessary to obtain gauge. It is very important to knit to gauge otherwise the garment will be too big or too small.

BODY: Using smaller circular needle and Medium Violet, cast on 174 (192, 216, 244, 270, 286, 298, 324) stitches. Knit in the round for 1¼ inches for the hem, purl 1 round, knit 1¼ inches. Change to larger needle and Dark Charcoal, and increase to 198 (220, 264, 286, 308, 330, 352, 374) stitches evenly spaced. Work the pattern according to Border 1. When the pullover measures 13¾ (15¾, 18½, 21¼, 21¾, 22½, 22¾, 23½) inches, shape for the front neck: For the center front, bind off 30 (34, 38, 42, 42, 42, 46, 46) stitches. Work back and forth until the garment measures 15¼ (17¾, 20½, 22¾, 23¼, 24, 24¾, 25½) inches. To shape the back neck, bind off in the same way as you did for the front neck. Work each side separately until the pullover measures 16¼ (18, 21, 24, 24¾, 25½, 26½, 26¾) inches. Put the stitches on a holder.

SLEEVES: Using smaller double-point needles and Medium Violet, cast on 38 (40, 44, 50, 54, 56, 56, 60) stitches. Knit in the round. Work the hem as you did the body. Change to larger needles and Dark Charcoal, and increase to 60 (60, 64, 64, 68, 76, 72, 80) stitches evenly spaced. Work the pattern according to the graph, and at the same time, increase 2 stitches (1 at the beginning, and 1 at the end of the round) every 3 (3, 3, 3, 3, 3, 2, 2) rounds until you have 120 (138, 148, 156, 168, 176, 200, 210) stitches. Knit until the sleeve measures 13¾ (15¾, 18½, 20½, 20½, 20, 20, 20) inches. To make the facing that covers up the cut edge: purl 1 round, knit 7 rounds, and bind off.

FINISHING: Mark, stitch, and cut the sleeve openings (see Finishing, page 134). Graft the shoulders. Using smaller needle and Medium Violet, pick up stitches around the neck. Knit 4 rounds decreasing 1 stitch at each corner every round. Purl 1 round, then knit 4 rounds increasing 1 stitch at each corner every round. Bind off. Sew in the sleeves. Sew the hems and the facings to the purl side. Weave all the loose ends into the back of the fabric. Steam lightly.

BERET: Using smaller circular needle and Medium Violet, cast on 154 stitches. Knit in the round for 1¼ inches for the hem, purl 1 round, and knit 4 rounds. Work one pattern repeat. Change to larger needle and Dark Charcoal, and increase as follows: *Knit 4 stitches, increase 1*, repeat between *'s around. Knit 6 rounds even. Next round: *Knit 5 stitches, increase 1*, repeat between *'s around. Knit 6 rounds even.

Purl 1 round, knit 6 rounds, then decrease as follows:

Knit 5 stitches, knit 2 together, repeat between *'s around.

Knit 6 rounds even.

Knit 4 stitches, knit 2 together, repeat between *'s around.

Knit 6 rounds even.

Knit 3 stitches, knit 2 together, repeat between *'s around.

Knit 6 rounds even.

Knit 2 stitches, knit 2 together, repeat between *'s around.

Knit 6 rounds even.

Knit 1 stitch, knit 2 together, repeat between *'s around.

Next round: Knit 2 together around. Put the remaining stitches onyarn and gather. Sew the hem to the purl side. Weave all loose ends into the back of the fabric. Steam lightly.

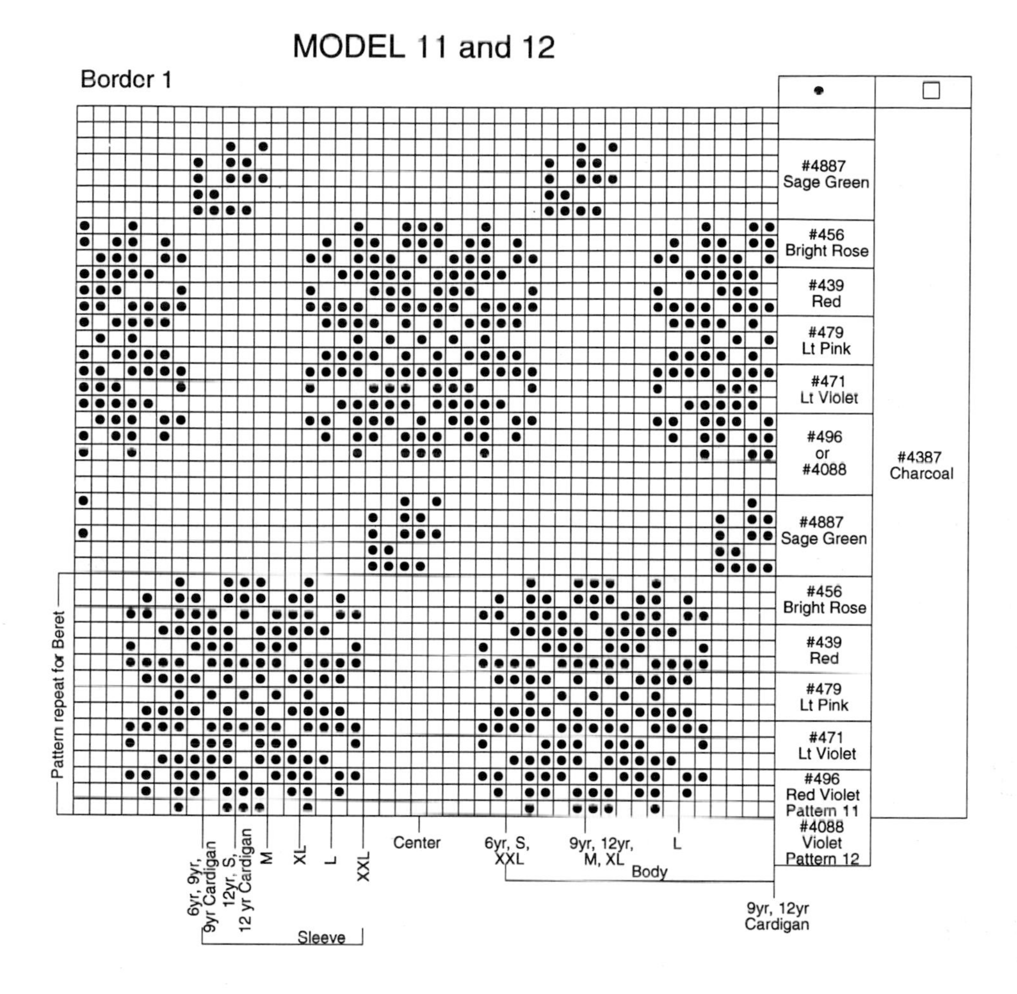

MODEL 11

Border 2

•	□
#4385 Lt Blue	#4387 Charcoal
#4887 Sage Green	#467 Midnight Blue
#496 Red Violet	#4387 Charcoal
#456 Bright Rose	
#439 Red	
#479 Lt Pink	
#471 Lt Violet	#467 Midnight
#496 Red Violet	#4387 Charcoal
#4887 Sage Green	#467 Midnight Blue
#4385 Lt Blue	#4387 Charcoal

Center

MODEL 13

A BLUE DREAM

On this sweater, the designs are placed in a fairly traditional way, with borders at the bottom of the body and the sleeves, and a surface design that covers the rest. The colors make a big difference on this sweater. The main color in the borders consists of several green and blue shades, and the contrast color is constantly changing, as well. The body design is more calm. A dark purple color clearly shows the design against a background that alternates between purple/ blue and green/blue. Some of the green and pink colors are very bright and strong. If the whole garment was to be made in such strong colors, it could easily look gaudy. As long as the strongest colors are used carefully, they only add life and sparkle to the general impression.

YARN: Rauma Finullgarn. The sweater shown is knit in the colors listed below.

CHART: page 96

SIZES: 6 yrs (9 yrs, 12 yrs, S, M, L, XL, XXL)

COLORS: #474 Deep Violet–200 (250, 250, 300, 300, 350, 400, 450)g; #4385 Medium Blue–50 (50, 50, 100, 100, 100, 150, 150)g; #472 Light Blue–100 (100, 150, 150, 200, 200, 200, 250)g; #437 Blue–50g; #4886 Cyclamen–50g; #4686 Hot Pink–50g; #478 Medium Rose–50g; #430 Green–50g; #494 Dark Green–50g; #458 Medium Green–50g; #493 Light Sage Green–50g; #419 Medium Rust–50g.

GAUGE: 27 stitches and 32 rounds =4 × 4 inches

NEEDLE SUGGESTION: Circular and double-point knitting needles size 2.5mm and 3mm, or size necessary to obtain gauge. It is very important to knit to gauge otherwise the garment will be too big or too small.

BODY: Using smaller circular needle and Deep Violet, cast on 168 (196, 224, 252, 266, 280, 308, 336) stitches. Join and knit 12 rounds for the hem, purl 1 round, then knit Border 1 according to the graph. Change to larger needle and increase to 192 (240, 240, 288, 288, 336, 336, 384) stitches evenly spaced. Knit Borders 2 and 3, increasing to 216 (240, 264, 288, 312, 336, 360, 384) stitches evenly spaced on the last round of Border 3. Continue in Border 4. Work until the garment measures 13¾ (15¾, 18½, 21¼, 21½, 22½, 22¾, 23½) inches. Bind off the center front 26 (30, 34, 38, 38, 38, 42, 42) stitches for the neck opening. Work back and forth until the pullover measures 15½ (17¾, 20½, 22¾, 23¼, 24, 24¾ 25½) inches. To shape the back neck, bind off in the same way as you did for the front neck. Finish the two sides separately working back and forth. Work until the garment measures 16¼ (18¼, 20⅞, 24, 24¾, 25½, 26½, 26¾) inches. Put the stitches on a holder.

SLEEVES: The sleeves have the same design and colors as the body. Using smaller double-point needles and Deep Violet, cast on 38 (40, 44, 50, 54, 56, 56, 60) stitches. Knit in the round. Knit the hem and Border 1 as you did the body. Change to larger needles, and increase to 60 (64, 64, 64, 68, 76, 70, 80) stitches evenly spaced. Continue working Borders 2, 3, and 4, beginning at the point shown on the graph, and at the same time, increase 2 stitches (1 stitch at the beginning, and 1 stitch at the end of the round) every 3 (3, 3, 3, 3, 3, 2, 2) rounds until you have 120 (138, 148, 156, 168, 176, 200, 210) stitches on the needles. Knit until the sleeve measures 13¾ (15¾, 18½, 20⅞, 20½, 20, 19½, 19¼) inches. To make the facing that covers up the cut edge: purl 1 round, knit 7 rounds, and bind off.

FINISHING: Mark, stitch, and cut the sleeve openings (see Finishing, page 134). Graft the shoulders. Using Deep Violet, pick up stitches around the neck. Knit 1 round, purl 1 round, and knit 5 rounds increasing 1 stitch at each corner every round. Bind off. Sew in the sleeves. Sew all the facings to the wrong side. Weave all loose ends into the back of the fabric. Steam lightly.

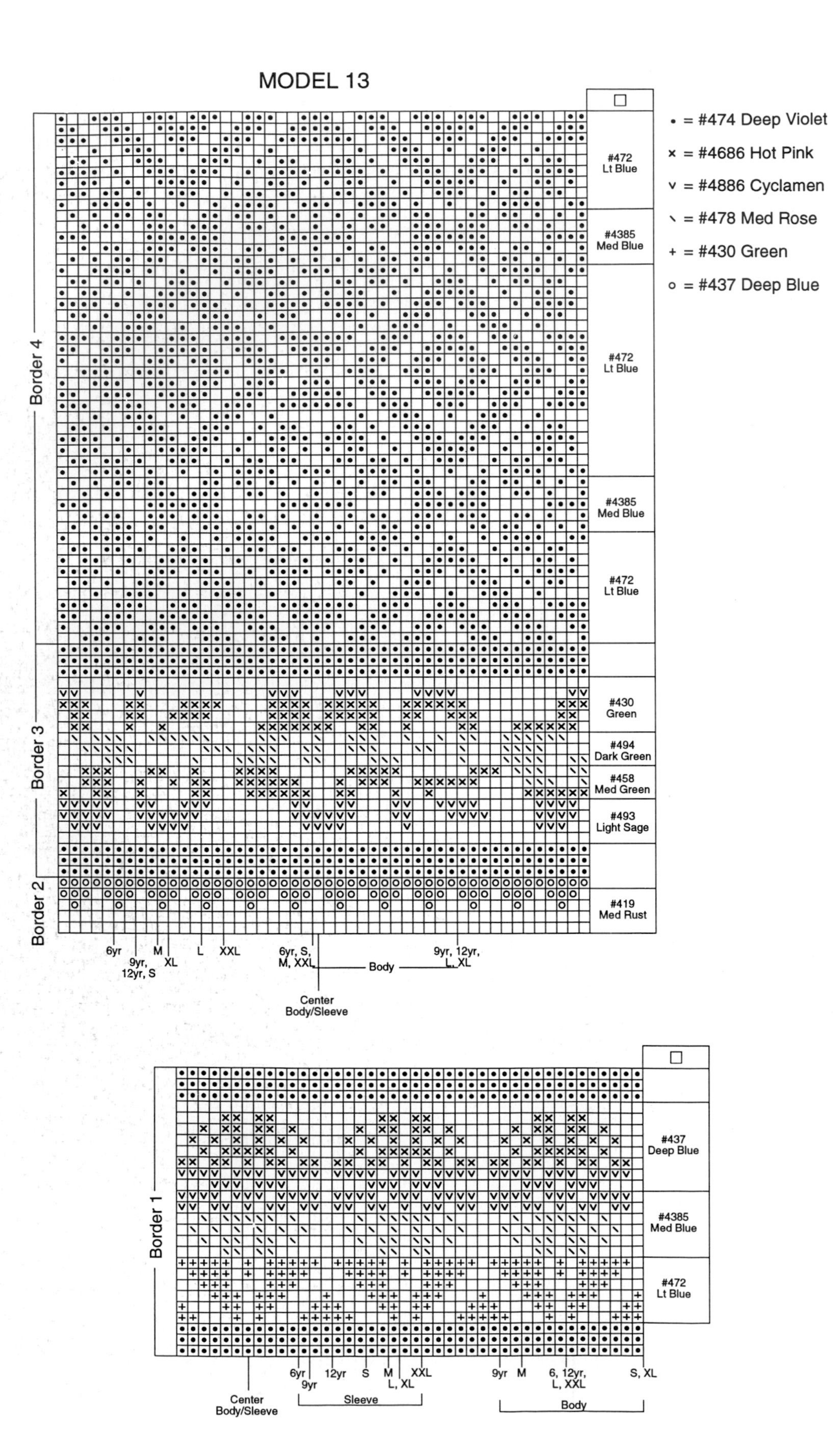
MODEL 13
• = #474 Deep Violet
× = #4686 Hot Pink
v = #4886 Cyclamen
ˎ = #478 Med Rose
+ = #430 Green
o = #437 Deep Blue
#472 Lt Blue
#4385 Med Blue
#472 Lt Blue
#4385 Med Blue
#472 Lt Blue
#430 Green
#494 Dark Green
#458 Med Green
#493 Light Sage
#419 Med Rust
Border 4
Border 3
Border 2
6yr
9yr, 12yr, S
M
XL
L
XXL
6yr, S, M, XXL
Body
9yr, 12yr, L, XL
Center Body/Sleeve
#437 Deep Blue
#4385 Med Blue
#472 Lt Blue
Border 1
Center Body/Sleeve
6yr
9yr
12yr
S
M
L, XL
XXL
Sleeve
9yr
M
6, 12yr, L, XXL
S, XL
Body

WHEN THE DESIGN IS DETERMINED BY THE SHAPE

One of the advantages of making your own designs is that you can adjust them to the particular garment you are knitting. The designs can, for instance, be made so that they are practical to knit whenever you have to decrease and shape a garment. They can also be made to emphasize certain parts of a garment, such as the neck, sleeves, or back. This is easy to do. For example, the following design and sketch show a simple sweater with set-in sleeves. The main design on the sleeves and the body is light and plain. The borders at the bottom and the center front are related, but they are more complex than the body design. Still, the borders and the body design are well integrated in this sweater.

These design fragments are planned as sweater decoration around V-necks, round necks, and boat necks. The straight borders are to be used at the bottom of the sleeves and body.

MODEL 14a

AN A-SHAPED CARDIGAN AND TIGHTS

This cardigan is A-shaped, meaning it is wider at the bottom than at the top. First, we figured out how many stitches we had to bind off for the shape to be correct, then we designed the stars accordingly. The stars are quite big at the bottom, and they get smaller and smaller towards the yoke.

The wool tights are knitted in a diagonal square design. It probably would have been too much to use the star design here as well. The square design, on the other hand, emphasizes the stars.

YARN: Rauma Finullgarn. The sweater shown is knit in the colors listed below.

CHARTS: 101–102

SIZE: One size

COLORS: #434 Light Rust–100g; #488 Brick–400g; #476 Medium Earth Green–50g; #498 Light Yellow Green–50g; #486 Earth Green–100g; #409 Medium Brick–50g; #440 Wooden Rose–50g; #490 Dusky Rose–50g; #470 Dark Lilac–100g; #427 Medium Lilac–150g; #473 Light Lilac–50g.

GAUGE: 27 stitches and 32 rounds = 4 × 4 inches

NEEDLE SUGGESTION: Circular knitting needles (extra-long circular needles are available for oversized garments like this one) size 3mm, or size necessary to obtain gauge. It is very important to knit to gauge otherwise the garment will be too big or too small.

BODY: Using Light Rust, cast on 452 stitches. Knit in the round. Purl the first 3 stitches all the time, using a double strand These 3 stitches will be machine stitched and cut open later on for the front opening. Knit 3/4 inch for the hem, purl 4 rounds and knit 2 rounds. Now start working the design according to the graph. The cardigan consists of 14 gussets getting narrower as you work your way up. The decreases are marked on the graphs and take place on each side of a vertical row of brick-colored stitches between the gussets. Work Border 1, then Border 2, decreasing on the first round for the gussets, then Border 3, again decreasing for the gussets on the first round. The decreases are worked between each row of stars. Finally the gussets melt together to a star yoke, and the vertical rows of brick-colored stitches are eliminated. Of the 14 gussets, 8 are on the back, and 3 are on each of the two fronts, leaving room for the collar. Knit and decrease according to the graphs until Border 3 is completed. Put the stitches on a holder.

SLEEVES: Using Light Rust, cast on 64 stitches. Knit in the round. Work the lower edge as for the body. Knit the 1st star according to Border 1. Using Brick, knit 1 round, increasing to 80 stitches evenly spaced, and knit the stars as for the yoke in Border 3. At the same time, increase 2 stitches (1 stitch at the beginning and 1 stitch at the end of the round) every 3rd round until there are 168 stitches on the needle. Knit until the sleeve measures 20 inches. To make the facing that covers up the cut edge: purl 1 round, knit 7 rounds, and bind off.

FINISHING: Machine stitch and cut along the double-stranded purl stitches for front opening. Mark, stitch, and cut the sleeve openings (see Finishing, page 134). Remember to center 3 stars on each front and 8 stars on the back so you have room for the collar. Graft the shoulders. Using Brick, pick up stitches along the two front edges and around the neck. To determine how many stitches to pick up, measure up one front edge, around the neck, and back down the other front edge. Multiply this number of inches by the gauge (8 stitches per inch) and adjust this number to fit a multiple of 32 (the number of stitches in the pattern repeat) plus 1 for balance. After picking up these stitches, cast on 2 additional purl stitches before joining the round. These 2 stitches are to be stitched and cut later on. Knit the Collar graph. Using Light Rust, knit 2 rounds and purl 4 rounds. Continue working stripes alternating 1 Earth Green and 1 Brick for the inside (facing) of the collar. Match the length to the outside of the collar. Bind off. Machine stitch and cut the 2 purl stitches. Sew the corners of the collar from the purl side. Sew in the sleeves. Sew all the facings to the wrong side. Weave all loose ends into the back of the fabric. Steam lightly.

MODEL 14b

CHECKERED TIGHTS

YARN: Rauma Finullgarn. The tights shown are knit in the colors listed below.

SIZES: S (M, L)

COLORS:

#488 Brick–100g

#427 Medium Lilac–100g

#486 Earth Green–100g

#476 Medium Earth Green–100g

#434 Light Rust–50g

GAUGE: 27 stitches and 32 rounds = 4 × 4 inches

NEEDLE SUGGESTION: Circular and double point-knitting needles size 3mm, or size necessary to obtain gauge. It is very important to knit to gauge otherwise the garment will be too big or too small.

TIGHTS: Using double point needles and Light Rust, cast on 59 (63, 65) stitches for one leg. Knit in the round for 6 rounds for the hem, purl 1 round, and knit 4 rounds. Work according to the graph, and at the same time, increase 2 stitches (1 at the beginning, and 1 at the end of the round) every 5th round until you have 147 (151, 155) stitches on the needle. Continue until the leg measures 27¼ (28, 28¾) inches. Knit the other leg to match. Then bind off 15 stitches on the inside of each leg (at the inseam). Put the legs together, inseams facing each other, and put all the stitches on one circular needle. Continue working in the round. At the front, decrease 2 stitches (1 from each leg) every other round 5 times (10 stitches decreased). At the back, decrease 2 stitches every other round 9 times (18 stitches decreased). Depending on your placement of squares, you may need to decrease a few more stitches to make the pattern come out even at the center front and at the center back.

You can decrease a few more stitches to make it come out even. Work until the tights measure 37¾ (38½, 39½) inches. Change to Light Rust. Knit 1¼ inches for the casing, purl 1 round, knit 1¼ inches. Bind off. Sew the casing to the purl side and put in elastic. Hem the tights and sew the crotch seam. Weave all loose ends into the back of the fabric. Steam lightly.

BERET: Using smaller needle and Light Rust, cast on 156 stitches. Knit in the round for 8 rounds for the hem, purl 3 rounds and knit 2 rounds. Then knit the largest star on Border 1 with 1 stitch between each star in colors matching the cardigan. After the star, change to larger needle and work stripes alternating 1 stitch Medium Lilac and 1 stitch Brick. Increase 2 stitches 6 different places, i.e. on each side of the stitch between the stars. Increase this way every other round 5 times. Now decrease 2 stitches at the same 6 places every 3rd round 7 times, then decrease 2 stitches in the same 6 places every other round until you have 8 stitches left. Put the remaining stitches on a thread and gather. Hem and steam lightly.

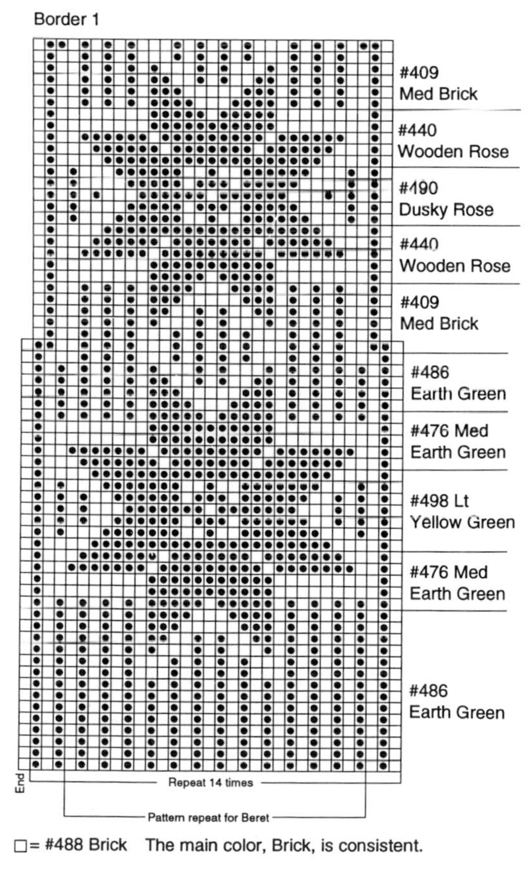

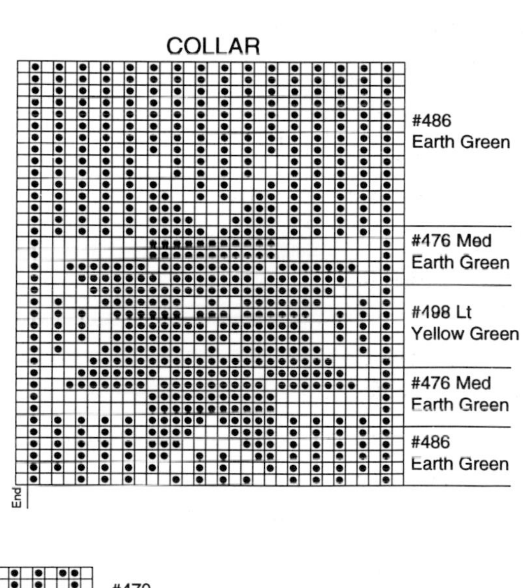

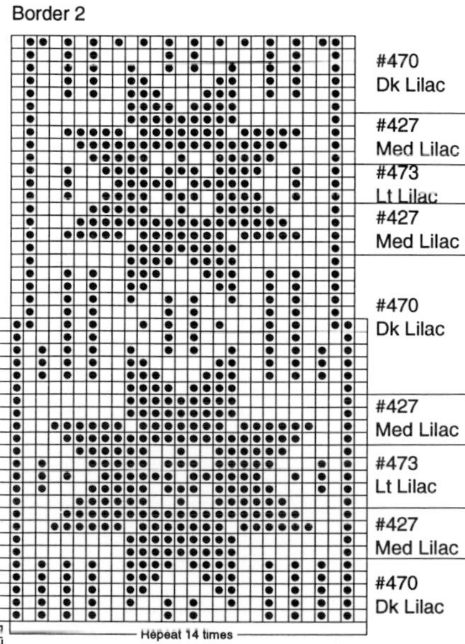

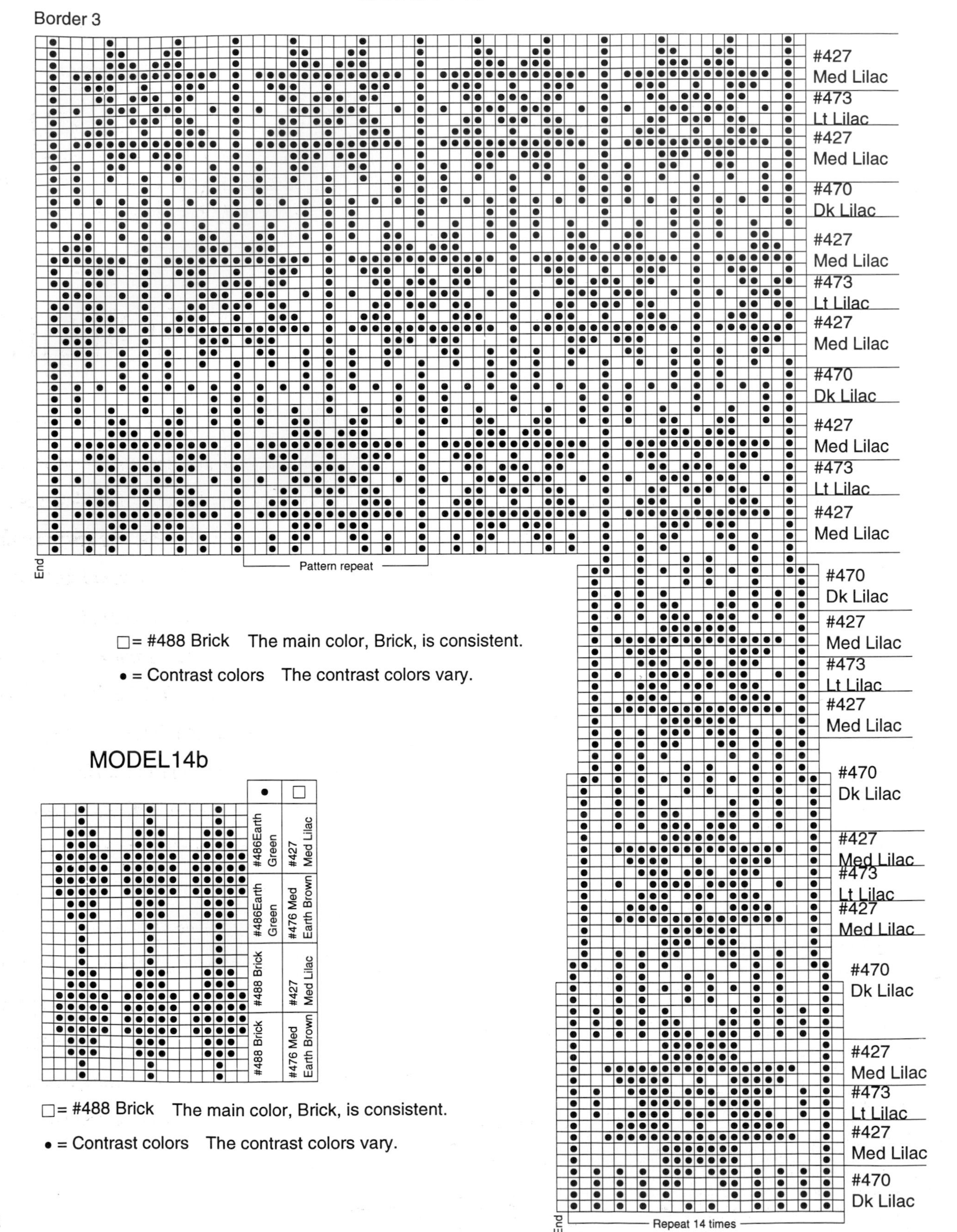
MODEL 14a
Border 3
#427 Med Lilac
#473 Lt Lilac
#427 Med Lilac
#470 Dk Lilac
#427 Med Lilac
#473 Lt Lilac
#427 Med Lilac
#470 Dk Lilac
#427 Med Lilac
#473 Lt Lilac
#427 Med Lilac
End
Pattern repeat
#470 Dk Lilac
#427 Med Lilac
#473 Lt Lilac
#427 Med Lilac
#470 Dk Lilac
#427 Med Lilac
#473 Lt Lilac
#427 Med Lilac
#470 Dk Lilac
#427 Med Lilac
#473 Lt Lilac
#427 Med Lilac
#470 Dk Lilac
End
Repeat 14 times
□= #488 Brick The main color, Brick, is consistent.
• = Contrast colors The contrast colors vary.
MODEL14b
•
□
#486Earth Green
#427 Med Lilac
#486Earth Green
#476 Med Earth Brown
#488 Brick
#427 Med Lilac
#488 Brick
#476 Med Earth Brown
□= #488 Brick The main color, Brick, is consistent.
• = Contrast colors The contrast colors vary.

MODEL 15

BIRD SWEATER WITH CABLE DESIGN AND EMBROIDERY

The stripes in this sweater are actually narrow cables worked in red and black. At the front is a triangle of birds. The stripe cables are a small, somewhat indistinct design, in which the colors seem to blend. There are much bigger areas of color in the bird design, which explains why that part of the sweater stands out. The edges are knit borders with embroidery. A sweater with nothing but striped cables would be boring, and the bird triangle by itself would not be as attractive. Together, the two designs interact in an exciting look. The bird triangle adds some dynamics to the simple square shape of the sweater, a composition

you do not get tired of looking at. The triangle is almost a "challenge" to the square it sits upon.

YARN: Rauma Finullgarn. The sweater shown is knit in the colors listed below.

CHARTS: pages 104–105

SIZES: M (L, XL, XXL)

COLORS: #436 Black–300 (350, 400, 450)g; #499 Light Burgundy–250 (300, 350, 400)g; #484 Medium Turquoise–100 (100, 150, 150)g; #434 Light Rust–100 (100, 100, 100)g

GAUGE: 27 stitches and 32 rounds = 4 × 4 inches

NEEDLE SUGGESTION: Circular and double-point knitting needles size 2.5mm and 3mm, or size necessary to obtain gauge. It is very important to knit to gauge otherwise the garment will be too big or too small.

TWO-COLOR CABLE: A.*Knit stripes alternating 1 stitch each of Black and Light Burgundy for 5 rounds. Slip the Black stitch onto a cable needle to the front of the work, knit the Light Burgundy stitch, then knit the Black stitch on the cable needle*. Repeat between *'s around. B. Knit stripes for 5 rounds in established pattern. *Slip the Light Burgundy stitch onto a cable needle to the back of the work, knit the Black stitch, then the Light Burgundy stitch on the cable needle*. Repeat between *'s around. Repeat both A and B. When you cross a cable pattern over 2 stitches, it is very important that you are consistent in crossing the colors in the right direction.

BODY: Using smaller circular needle and Medium Turquoise, cast on 272 (288, 304, 320) stitches. Knit in the round for 2¼ inches for the hem, purl 1 round, then work Border 1. Change to larger needle and Black. Increase to 302 (326, 354, 386) stitches evenly spaced. Knit 3 rounds before starting the bird and cable patterns. The bird pattern goes over 151 stitches on the front. That leaves 0 (6, 13, 21) stitches on each side of the birds for cables. The back of the sweater is all cables. Work the birds and cables according to the graph until the garment measures 24 (24¾, 25½, 26 inches) from the purl round. Now work knit 1, purl 1 ribbing using Black for 3/4 inch. Bind off.

SLEEVES: Using smaller double-point needles and Medium Turquoise, cast on 48 (48, 64, 64) stitches. Knit in the round. Knit the hem as you did the body, then work Border 1. Change to larger needles and increase to 69 (77, 71, 81) stitches evenly spaced. Using Black, knit 3 rounds and then begin the cables, keeping the last "seam stitch" in Black. At the same time, increase 1 stitch in pattern on each side of the seam stitch every 3rd round until you have 95 (97, 99, 101) stitches on the needles. Then increase 1 stitch on each side of the seam stitch in pattern every round until you have 177 (193, 209, 225) stitches. When the sleeve measures 18½ (18⅞, 19¼, 19¼) inches, knit 3 rounds using Black, then work Border 1 from the top down. To make the facing that covers up the cut edge, purl 1 round, knit 7 rounds. Bind off.

FINISHING: Mark, sew, and cut the sleeve openings (see Finishing, page 134). Graft the shoulders and sew in the sleeves. The boat neck is 11¾ (12¼, 12½, 13) inches wide. Using Black, embroider chain stitches around each star along the edges. Sew all the facings to the wrong side. Weave all loose ends into the back of the fabric. Steam lightly.

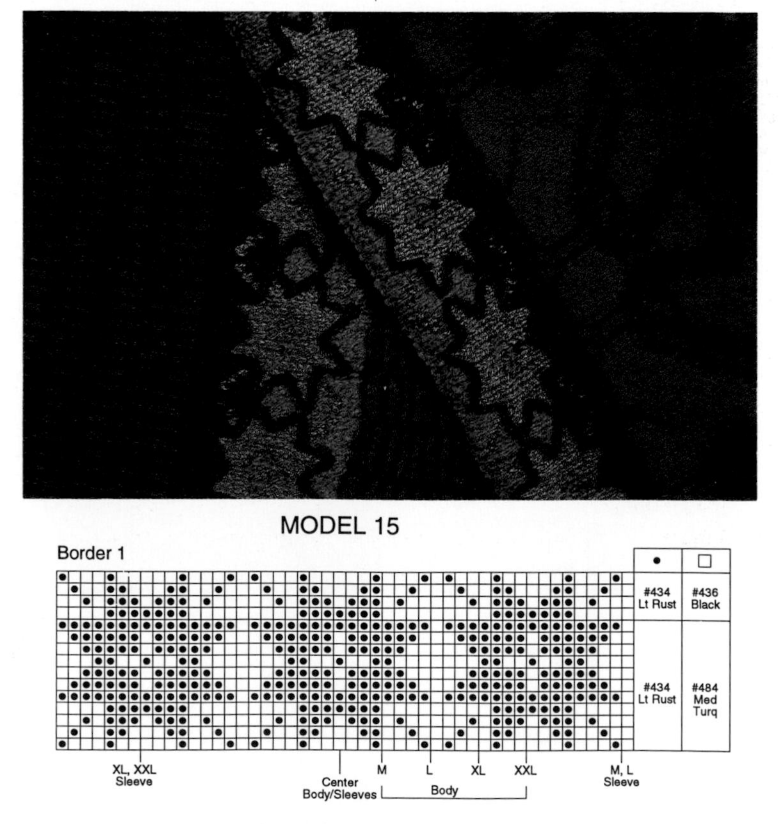

Work pattern from top to bottom for top of sleeve.

Border 2

□ = #499 Light Burgundy

• = #436 Black

⁄ = place previous Lt Burgundy st on cable needle to back, knit Black st, then knit st on cable needle.

⁍ = place Black st on cable needle to front, knit next Lt Burgundy st, then knit st on cable needle.

MODEL 16

BOLERO WITH ROSE-PAINTED BACK

This cardigan is knitted on circular needles from wrist to wrist, except for the back with the large acanthus border, which is worked back and forth. There is only one contrast color, and one main color in the floral motif. The stem and the outlining are embroidered on as a finish. The bolero looks good with a fur collar, if that is your taste . . .

YARN: Rauma Finullgarn. The sweater shown is knit in the colors listed below.

CHART: page 109

SIZE: One size

COLORS: #436 Black–350g; #447 Light Navy–50g; #434 Light Rust–50g; #470 Dark Lilac–100g; #497 Red Wine–100g; #499 Light Burgundy–50g; #444 Deep Rust–50g; #498 Light Yellow Green–50g

GAUGE: 27 stitches and 32 rounds = 4 × 4 inches

NEEDLE SUGGESTION: Circular and double-point knitting needles size 3mm, or size necessary to obtain gauge. It is very important to knit to gauge otherwise the garment will be too big or too small.

BOLERO: Using double-point needles and Black, cast on 55 stitches for the first sleeve. Knit in the round for 8 rounds for the hem, purl 1 round and knit 1 round. Work Borders 1, 2, and 3 according to the graph. At the same time, after working Border 1 for 1½ inches, increase 1 stitch at the beginning, and 1 stitch at the end of the round every 3rd round until you have 93 stitches. Then increase 2 stitches every round until you have 155 stitches, and 2 stitches every other round until you have 209 stitches. Cast on 3 new stitches over the first stitch on the round, and purl these stitches every round, using a double strand when possible. These stitches are to be machine stitched and cut open later on for the waist opening. Continue to increase 1 stitch on each side of the purl stitches every 3rd round until you have 240 stitches (including the 3 purl stitches). Finish Border 3 and then knit Border 4 to the front opening. Bind off 128 stitches for the front opening (including the 3 purl stitches). The next 37 rows form the center back of the bolero and have to be worked back and forth. Then cast on 128 stitches (including the 3 purl stitches). Finish working the front opening, then Border 3, Border 2, and Border 1, matching the other side, and decreasing the same way you increased on the opposite side: Decrease 1 stitch on each side of the purl stitches every 3rd round until you have 212 stitches. Bind off the 3 purl stitches, and work the other sleeve to match. Decrease 2 stitches every other round until you have 155 stitches, then decrease 2 stitches every round until you have 93 stitches, and 2 stitches every 3rd round until 55 stitches are left on the needles. Knit for 1½ inches. Border 1 is complete. With Black, knit 1 round, purl 1 round. Knit for 1½ inches, and finish with the hem as the first sleeve.

FINISHING: Machine stitch and cut along the double-stranded purl stitches at the waistline of the bolero (see Finishing, page 134). Knit a facing around the entire sweater. Using Black, pick up stitches along one front, around the neck, along the other front, and along the lower edge. Knit 1 round, purl 1 round, then knit 8 rounds decreasing 1 stitch every round at the lower front corners. Increase 1 stitch at each shoulder, and increase 2 stitches on each side seam every round. This makes the facing lay flat. Bind off. Sew all the facings to the wrong side. Weave all loose ends into the back of the fabric. Steam lightly.

To finish off, strengthen the center back motif by doing some embroidery. Using Light Rust and chain stitches, sew around the flower. Using Light Navy, Light Rust and Light Yellow Green, sew stem stitches according to the close up picture on page 108. To work a stem stitch, pass over a knit stitch, pull through to the purl side, go under the next knit stitch, and come up on the knit side. Then go back to the purl side in the same hole as the previous stitch ended.

A chain stitch is made by coming up to the knit side and going down to the purl side in the same hole, leaving a loop on the knit side. When you make the next stitch coming up and going down in the same hole, make sure you also come up inside the loop you left on the knit side, and pull the thread. Finally, you can sew on some fur around the edge.

BERET: Using smaller circular needle and Deep Rust, cast on 155 stitches. Join and Knit in the round for 1¼ inches, purl 1 round, and knit 3 rounds. Now knit the same acanthus design as you did along the fronts. The design is knit in Red Wine. Complete the acanthus design, and then knit 2 rounds with Black. Change to larger needle and increase as follows:

Knit 4 stitches, increase 1, repeat between *'s around. Knit 6 rounds.

Next round: *Knit 5 stitches, increase 1*, repeat between *'s around.

Knit 6 rounds. Purl 1 round, knit 6 rounds.

Now decrease as follows:

Knit 5 stitches, Knit 2 together, repeat between *'s around. Knit 6 rounds.

Next: *Knit 4 stitches, knit 2 together*, repeat between *'s around. Knit 6 rounds.

Next: *Knit 3 stitches, knit 2 together*, repeat between *'s around.

Knit 6 rounds.

Next: *Knit 2 stitches, knit 2 together*, repeat between *'s around. Knit 5 rounds.

Next: *Knit 1 stitch, knit 2 together*, repeat between *'s around.

Next: Knit 2 stitches together around. Put the remaining stitches on yarn and gather. Weave all loose ends into the back of the fabric. Steam lightly.

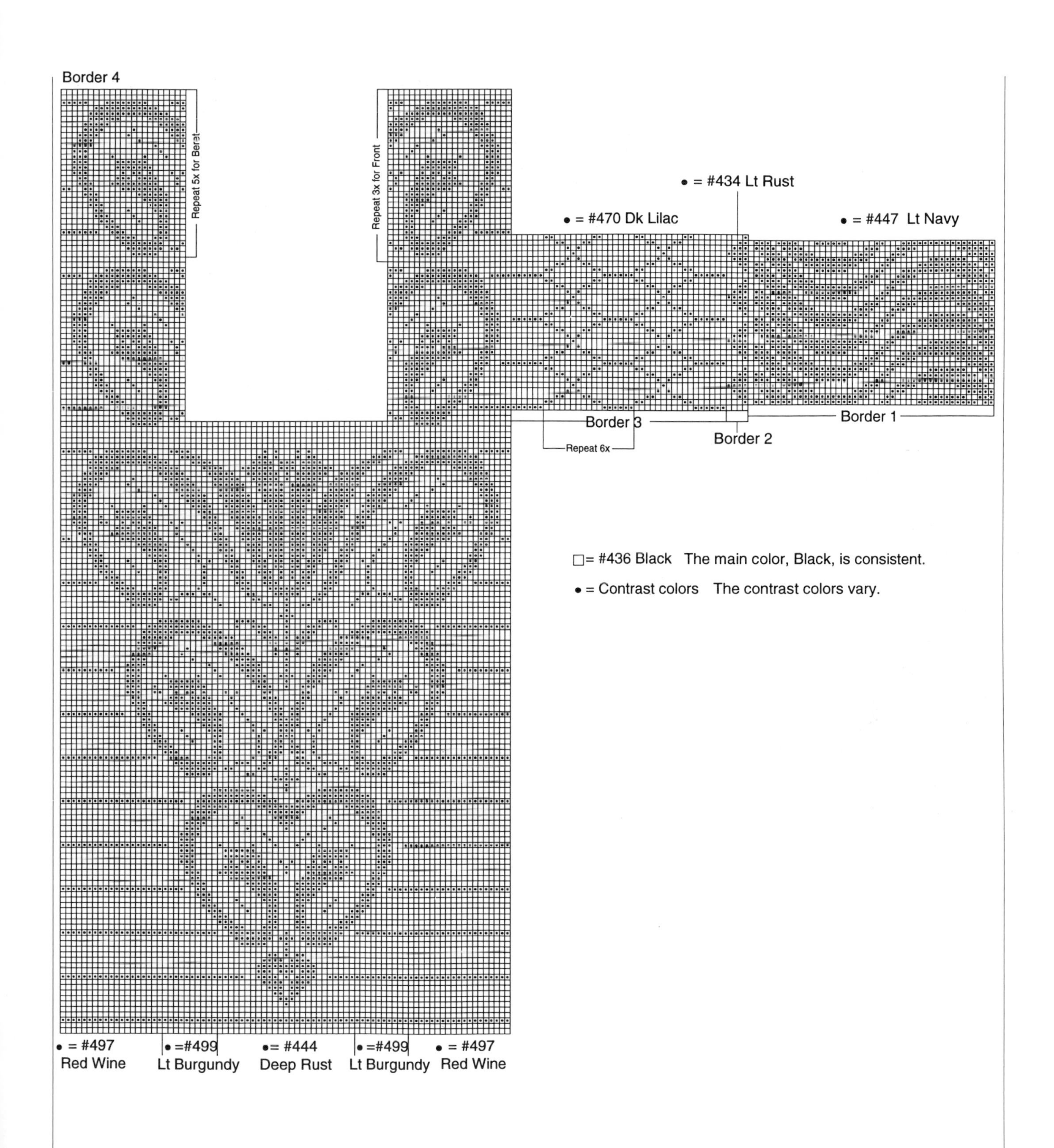
Border 4
Repeat 5x for Beret
Repeat 3x for Front
• = #434 Lt Rust
• = #470 Dk Lilac
• = #447 Lt Navy
Border 3
Repeat 6x
Border 2
Border 1
□= #436 Black The main color, Black, is consistent.
• = Contrast colors The contrast colors vary.
• = #497 Red Wine
• =#499 Lt Burgundy
•= #444 Deep Rust
• =#499 Lt Burgundy
• = #497 Red Wine

THAT LITTLE EXTRA

We hope you have found some useful tips and motivation while reading this book. Designs and colors are just a couple of areas within the world of knitting. There are still a great many others to explore, such as using materials other than wool; making designs of knit and purl stitches (for example, purl the contrast color squares and knit the main color squares); using embroidery, beads, or lace; and making cable designs.

We just want to point out a few of the endless possibilities for making exciting clothing, and hope that you will want to continue experimenting on your own. Our motto for this section is "Anything Goes!" Think of what you can do with just a few needles and yarn! And even if we have said it before, it does not hurt to repeat it: Do not let unsuccessful experiments stop you. You learn as much from your mistakes as from you successes, as long as you are open to new possibilities. So be patient and do not give up, even when something does not seem to work right away; you might be able to use the idea later, in a different project. The exciting kingdom of knitting lays open in front of you.

MODEL 17

A CARDIGAN WITH ROSES, BEADS, AND RUFFLES

This cardigan has color variations both in the leaf and rose designs. Sewn on, the beads appear like small "lice". On the leaves, the beads are turquoise and green, and related to the colors of the design. On the roses, the copper-colored beads look more like the background color.

YARN: Rauma Finullgarn. The sweater knit is shown in the colors listed below.

Beads: light green, turquoise, and copper

CHART: page 114

SIZE: S (L)

COLORS: #464 Brown–300g; #466 Rose–100g; #4571 Pink–50g; #4087 Light Rose–50g; #458 Medium Green–100g; #455 Light Green–100g; #431 Medium Gold–50g

GAUGE: 27 stitches and 32 rounds = 4 × 4 inches

NEEDLE SUGGESTION: Circular and double-point knitting needles size 3mm, or size necessary to obtain gauge. It is very important to knit to gauge otherwise the garment will be too big or too small.

BODY: Using Brown and circular needle, cast on 242 (290) stitches. Knit in the round. Purl the first 2 stitches on the round using a double strand on every round. They are to be machine stitch and cut for the front opening later on. Knit 8 rounds and then begin the charted design. Note that there are increases along each side of the cardigan. These increases are worked on each side of the Brown stitch that separates the flowers along the cardigan "side seams".

Work the design according to the graph, and increase 2 stitches on each side every other round until you have 290 (338) stitches. Work even until the cardigan measures 8 1/4 (9) inches. Now shape for the armholes on each side as follows: Bind off 3 stitches. On the next round cast on 2 new stitches over the bound-off stitches. Purl the new stitches using a double strand on every round. They are to be machine stitched and cut open later on. Continue working in the round, and do the armhole shaping on each side of the purl stitches: Decrease 1 stitch on each side every 3rd round until you have decreased 11 times (44 stitches decreased total). Work even until the garment measures 16 1/4 (17) inches. Shape for the front neck: Bind off the 20 center front stitches (includes the 2 purl stitches). You will have 224 (272) stitches remaining. Work back and forth decreasing 1 stitch on each side of the neck every other row. Decrease a total of 11 times until 202 (250) stitches remain. When the cardigan measures 18 (19) inches, bind off for back neck as you did for the front neck. Work 3/4 inch and place stitches on holder.

SLEEVES: Using double-point needles and Brown, cast on 50 stitches. Knit in the round for 8 rounds, then increase to 91 stitches evenly spaced. Work pattern according to the graph, and at the same time, increase 2 stitches (1 at the beginning and 1 at the end of the round) every 3rd round until you have 179 stitches. Continue knitting until the sleeve measures 19 1/4 (20) inches. To make the facing that covers up the cut edge: purl 1 round, knit 7 rounds, and bind off.

FINISHING: Machine stitch and cut along the double-stranded purl stitches for the front and armhole openings (see Finishing, page 134). Graft the shoulders. On the sleeves, make a pleat approximately 1 1/2 inches to each side of the shoulder seam. Adjust the pleats so that the sleeve fits the sleeve opening. Sew in the sleeve by hand or with a machine. Using Medium Gold, pick up stitches for the ruffle. Pick up the stitches along the front edges, along the lower edge and around the neck. Work in the round. Knit 2 rounds. Next round: *yarn over, knit 2 together, knit 3*, repeat between *'s around. Knit 1, (alternate 1 knit and 1 purl stitch) 3 times in each yarn over of the previous round. Purl the next round and bind off. Also knit ruffles along the sleeve edges. Sew all the facings to the wrong side. Weave all loose ends into the back of the fabric. Steam lightly. Finish by sewing the beads on using sewing thread. Sew turquoise and green beads on the leaves, and copper beads on the roses.

BERET: Using Medium Gold, cast on 144 stitches. Knit in the round for $1^1/_4$ inches. Next round: *Yarn over, knit 2 together*, repeat between *'s around. Knit 3 rounds. Change to Brown and knit 2 rounds before starting the pattern. Work 1 rose according to the graph. Then start increasing 1 stitch on each side of the Brown stitch between the roses. Increase every 3rd round 5 times. After completing the leaves, work with brown only. Knit, and decrease the same way as you increased every 3rd round 7 times. Then decrease the same way every other round until you have 12 stitches left. Put the remaining stitches on yarn and gather. Sew all the facings to the wrong side. Weave all loose ends into the back of the fabric. Steam lightly.

PATTERN 17

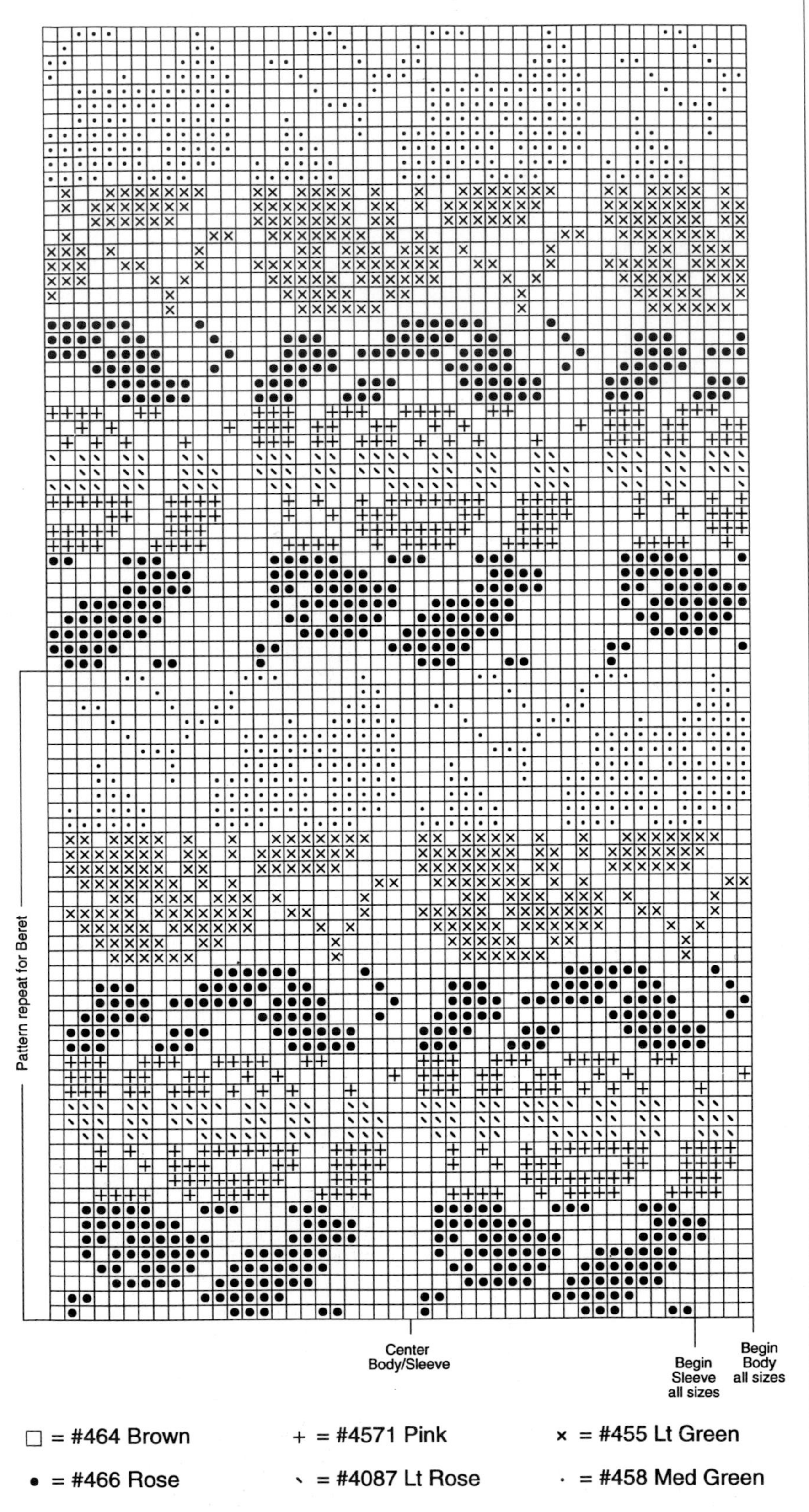

MODEL 18

SWEATER WITH BIRDS, CABLES, AND EMBROIDERY

We have used only two colors in knitting this sweater, and then enhanced the design by embroidery. The sleeves and the body have cables instead of regular ribbing.

YARN: Rauma Finullgarn. The sweater shown is knit in the colors listed below.

CHARTS: pages 116–117

SIZES: S (M, L, XL)

COLORS #438 Slate Blue–300 (300, 350, 400)g; #436 Black–300 (300, 350, 400)g; #498 Light Yellow Green–50g; #434 Light Rust–50g; #480 Burgundy–50g

GAUGE: 27 stitches and 32 rounds = 4 × 4 inches

NEEDLE SUGGESTION: Circular and double-point knitting needles size 2.5mm and 3mm, or size necessary to obtain gauge. It is very important to knit to gauge otherwise the garment will be too big or too small.

CABLES: Rounds 1-5: *Knit 4, purl 2*, repeat between *'s.

Round 6: *Put 2 stitches on a cable needle and hold to the front of the work, knit 2, then knit the 2 stitches from the cable needle, purl 2*, repeat between *'s around.

BODY: Using smaller circular needle and Black, cast on 240 (264, 288, 312) stitches. Knit in the round. Work cables as described for 4 inches ending on Round 3. Increase to 282 (298, 314, 352) stitches evenly spaced on last round. Change to larger needle and Slate Blue. Work the bird motif of Border 2 on the front 141 (149, 157, 173) stitches. Work Border 1 on the back 141 (149, 157, 173) stitches. Work until you have 4 (4, 5, 5) flowers at the center front. Then work ribbing; knit 1 through the back loop, purl 1 for 3/4 inch. Bind off.

SLEEVES: Using smaller double-point needles and Black, cast on 48 (54, 60, 60) stitches. Knit in the round. Work cables as you did the body. Change to larger needles and increase to 68 (68, 76, 68) stitches evenly spaced on last round. Start the round with 1 Black "seam stitch". Work Border 1 increasing 1 stitch in pattern on each side of the seam stitch every other round 0 (34, 36, 62) times, every 3rd round 44 (0, 0, 0) times, and every 4th round 0 (16, 14, 0) times. You will have 156 (168, 176, 200) stitches. Work even until the sleeve measures 20½ (20½, 20, 19½ inches). To make the facing that covers up the cut edge, purl 1 round, knit 7 rounds. Bind off.

FINISHING: Mark, stitch, and cut the sleeve openings (see Finishing, page 134). Graft the shoulders and sew in the sleeves. The boat neck is 11¾ (11¾, 12½, 12½) inches wide. Bind off. Sew all the facings to the wrong side. Weave all loose ends into the back of the fabric. Steam lightly.

Intensify the flowers by embroidery. Pass over a knit stitch, pull through to the purl side, go under the next knit stitch and come up on the knit side. Then go back to the purl side in the same hole as the previous stitch ended. Sew with red under the lower petal, and in the two blue points at the core. Use orange for the next two petals, and use both colors at the point of the flower. Use green along the stem.

BERET: Using smaller circular needle and Black, cast on 155 stitches. Knit in the round for 1¼ inches, purl 1 round, then knit 3 rounds increasing evenly to 160 stitches. Change to Slate Blue and knit 1 round before starting the pattern consisting of a repeat of the flower from the middle of the bird motif, with 1 stitch between the flowers. Finish the border by knitting 2 rounds of Slate Blue. Change to larger needle and Black, continue knitting, increasing as follows:

Knit 4, increase 1, repeat between *'s around.

Knit 6 rounds.

Next round: *Knit 5, increase 1*, repeat between *'s around.

MODEL 18

Border 1

End — Pattern repeat

□ = #438 Slate Blue

• = #436 Black

Knit 6 rounds. Purl 1 round, knit 6 rounds. Decrease as follows:

Knit 5, knit 2 together, repeat between *'s around. Knit 6 rounds.

Next round: *Knit 4, knit 2 together*, repeat between *'s around.

Knit 6 rounds.

Next round: *Knit 3, knit 2 together*, repeat between *'s around.

Knit 6 rounds.

Next round: *Knit 2, knit 2 together*, repeat between *'s around.

Knit 6 rounds.

Next round: *Knit 1, knit 2 together*, repeat between *'s around.

Next round: Knit 2 together around. Knit 6 rounds. Knit 2 together around. Knit 4 rounds. Put remaining stitches on yarn and gather. Sew all the facings to the wrong side. Weave all loose ends into the back of the fabric. Steam lightly. Embroider band to match the body.

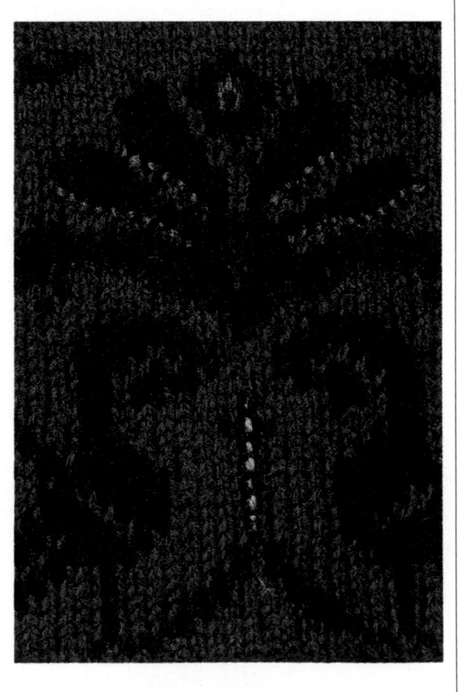

Border 2

□ = #438 Slate Blue
• = #436 Black

MODEL 19

SWEATER WITH FLOWER MOTIF, BEADS, AND "WOVEN" EDGES

In this design, you will find flowers, stars, and stripes. On the body, flowers top the long vines while the floral edge borders are done in a weaving technique. Beads enhance the center of each star. The sleeves are knitted in a stripe design, but because the stripes change color every so often, they give a square impression.

YARN: Rauma Finullgarn. The sweater shown is knit in the colors listed below.

CHARTS: pages 120–121

SIZES: S (M, L)

COLORS: #436 Black–200g; #458 Medium Green–100g; #439 Red–200 (250, 250)g; #4886 Cyclamen–50g; #461 Orange–150g; #485 Dark Turquoise–100g

GAUGE: 27 stitches and 32 rounds = 4 × 4 inches

NEEDLE SUGGESTION: Circular and double-point knitting needles size 2.5mm and 3mm, or size necessary to obtain gauge. It is very important to knit to gauge otherwise the garment will be too big or too small.

"WEAVE-KNIT": At the same time as you knit the background color, carry the contrast color to the front or to the back of the stitches you are knitting. The design shows up as you carry the contrast yarn to the front without knitting, across the knitted background stitch when the contrast color forms the design. Carry the contrast color to the back when the background color forms the design.

BODY: Using smaller circular needle and Black, cast on 252 (270, 288) stitches. Knit in the round for 2 1/4 inches for the hem, purl 1 round, then start Border 1 "weaving" according to the graph. Change to larger needle and Red. Increase to 266 (280, 294) stitches evenly spaced. Work Border 2. Then increase to 288 (304, 320) stitches evenly spaced. Work Border 3. In addition to the main pattern in Border 4, worked on the front and on the back, the sweater has vertical stripes on each side. The stripes consist of alternating 1 Red and 1 Medium Green stitch. Beginning at left side seam, knit 1 stitch in Medium Green ("seam stitch"), alternate 12 (2, 6) more stitches in Red and Medium Green. Work the flower motif over the next 117 (145, 145) stitches, work 27 (7, 15) vertical stripe stitches, work the flower motif over the next 117 (145, 145) stitches, work vertical stripe over next 14 (4, 8) stitches. There are 4 (5, 5) flowers on main panel. There are 6 (7, 8) small leaves on the stems. Complete the flower border, and knit Border 3 again. Put the 61 center front stitches on a holder. Work Border 5 back and forth for 1 1/2 inches. Work the same neck shaping on the back as you did for the front. Work another 1 1/4 inches. Place stitches on holder.

SLEEVES: Using smaller double-point needles and Black, cast on 54 stitches. Knit in the round. Work the hem and "woven" pattern in Border 1 as you did for the body. Change to larger needles and Red. Increase to 64 (68, 76) stitches evenly spaced and knit Border 2 at the same time as you increase 2 stitches (1 at the beginning and 1 at the end of the round) every other round. Work Border 3, then continue with Border 5. Knit and increase until you have 156 (168, 176) stitches total. Work even until the sleeve measures 20 1/2 (20, 20) inches. To make the facing that covers up the cut edge, purl 1 round, knit 7 rounds. Bind off.

FINISHING: Mark, stitch, and cut the sleeve openings (see Finishing, page 134). Graft the shoulders. Pick up stitches around the neck and work in the round. "Weave" the flower of Border 1, starting and ending with 2 rounds of one color. At the same time, decrease 1 stitch every round at each corner. Then purl 1 round, and knit 14 rounds increasing 1 stitch at each corner every round. Bind off. Sew in the sleeves. Sew all the facings to the wrong side. Weave all loose ends into the back of the fabric. Steam lightly. Finally, sew the black beads around the center of the stars in Border 2, and underline the petals in the flower motif by sewing a row of beads underneath it.

SQUARE BERET: Using smaller circular needle and Black, cast on 144 stitches. Knit in the round. Work the hem and the "woven" border as for the body. Change to larger needles, and work stripes alternating 1 Black and 1 Medium Green stitch, and at the same time increase 2 stitches 4 times every round; 1 stitch on each side of stitch number 36, 72, 108, and 144. The increased stitches are all worked in Black. Continue increasing for 20 rounds. Using Black, purl 1 round, then knit stripes, alternating 1 Black and 1 Red stitch. Decrease 2 stitches 4 times every round in the same manner as you increased until you have 8 stitches left. Put the remaining stitches on yarn and gather. Sew hem to the wrong side. Weave all loose ends into the back of the fabric. Steam lightly.

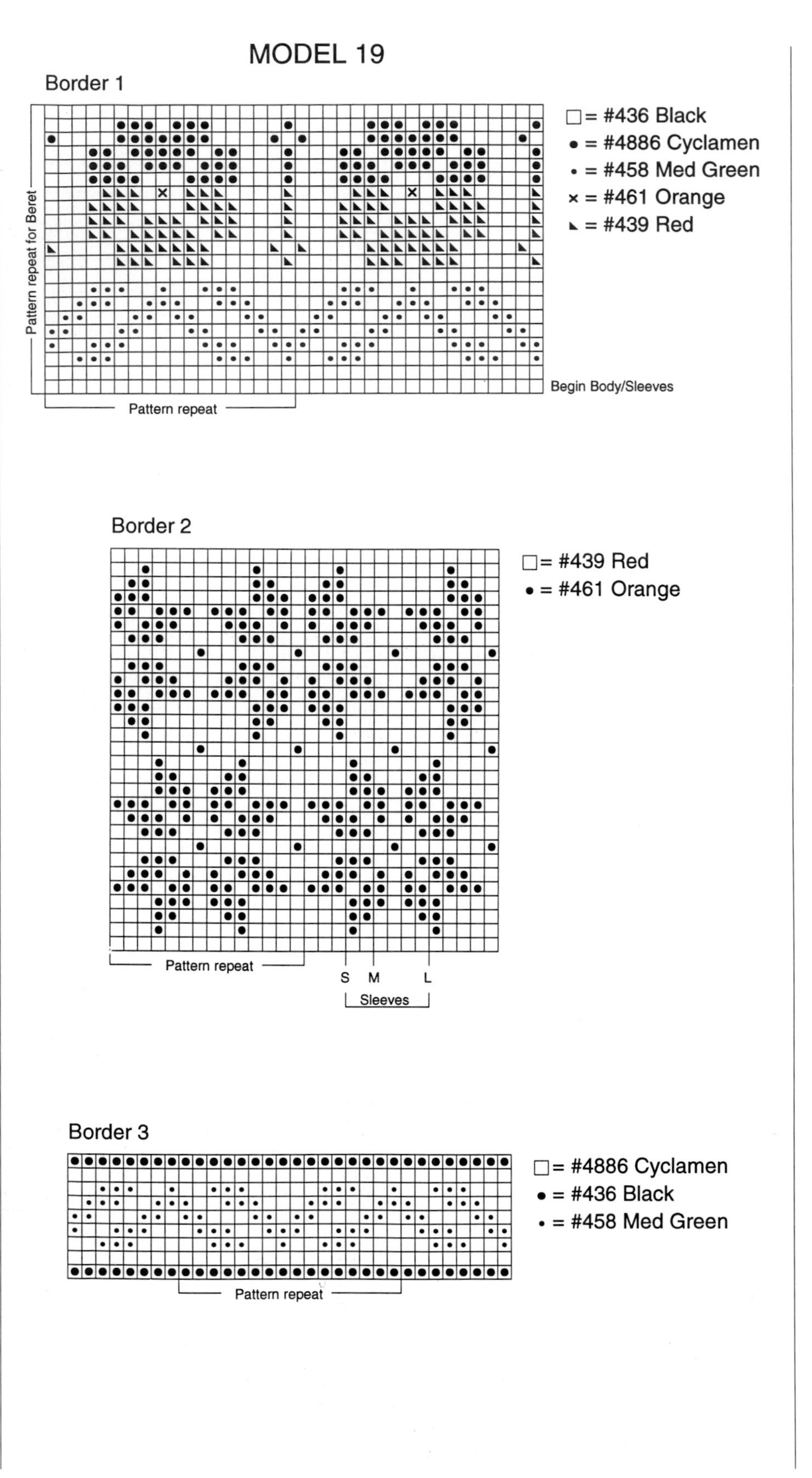

Border 4

Border 5

□ = #461 Orange
● = #439 Red
• = #458 Med Green
× = #436 Black

MODEL 20

SWEATER WITH CABLES AND RICH COLORS

What makes this sweater special is that the increases on the sleeves are hidden in the design. As the width of the sleeves increase, there are more and more purled stitches between each cable. The design itself forms the sleeves. The sweater is knitted from wrist to wrist. The lower edge of the sleeves and the body are knit in two colors. The main color is dark blue. In addition, there are two bright pink shades, two blue shades, and two bright green shades. The dark blue frames the other bright colors.

YARN: Rauma Finullgarn. The sweater shown is knit in the colors listed below.

CHART: page 124

SIZES: S (M, L)

COLORS: #459 Dark Navy–400g; #467 Midnight Blue–50g; #437 Blue–50g; #484 Medium Turquoise–100g; #483 Turquoise–100g; #499 Light Burgundy–100g; #456 Bright Rose–50g; #439 Red–50g

GAUGE: 27 stitches and 32 rounds = 4 × 4 inches

NEEDLE SUGGESTION: Circular and double-point knitting needles

size 3mm, or size necessary to obtain gauge. It is very important to knit to gauge otherwise the garment will be too big or too small.

CABLES:

Rounds 1–13: *Knit 6 stitches, purl 1 stitch*, repeat between *'s around.

Round 14: *Slip 3 stitches onto a cable needle and hold to the front of the work, knit 3, knit the stitches from the cable needle, purl 1*. Repeat between *'s around.

SWEATER: Using double-point needles and Dark Navy, cast on 54 stitches. Knit in the round for 1¼ inches for the hem, purl 1 round and knit 2 rounds. Change to Light Burgundy and knit 3 rounds. Knit Border 1 according to the graph. At the same time, increase 1 stitch at the beginning, and 1 stitch at the end of the round every 3rd round. After the border, knit 3 rounds using Light Burgundy. You will have 78 stitches. Change to Dark Navy and the cable pattern, and increase 27 stitches evenly spaced to 105 stitches. The cables go over 6 stitches with 1 purl stitch between each cable. NOTE: The sleeve increases will now take place between each cable (not as the regular underarm increases). Alternate the increases between the two sides of the purl panels between the cables. Work the cable pattern and increase 1 stitch in the purl stitch panel every 12th round, 9 times. Work until you have a total of 240 stitches. Mark the round. Then work the cables even until the garment measures 18 ¾ inches. Now divide your knitting at the underarm, and work cables back and forth until the garment measures 23½ (24½, 25½) inches. Work back and forth for 3 rows, decreasing to 224 stitches evenly spaced in 1 round. Cast on 2 new stitches at the lower edge of the sweater, and purl these 2 stitches on every round using both strands of yarn. They are to be sewn and cut open later on. Knit Border 2. The 2 stitches at the top (center) of the sleeve are worked in Dark Navy on every round. They will form the neck opening. From the lower edge, work as follows: Purl 2 stitches, knit 5 repeats of Border 2, purl 2 stitches (the 2 Dark Navy neck opening stitches), knit 5 repeats of Border 2. Complete Border 2, and finish by knitting 3 rounds of Dark Navy. Bind off the 2 purl stitches at the bottom of the sweater and increase to 240 stitches evenly spaced. Now work cables back and forth, for the same length as other side. Then join to a round again. Work to the same position where you finished increasing on the first sleeve. Start decreasing as follows: Decrease 1 stitch between the cables every 12th round until you have 15 cables and 1 purl stitch between the cables. You will have 105 stitches. Decrease 27 stitches evenly spaced to 78 stitches. Knit 3 rounds of Light Burgundy before knitting Border 1 reversed of the first sleeve. Decrease 2 stitches (1 at the beginning and 1 at the end of the round) every 3rd round to 54 stitches. Change to Light Burgundy and knit 3 rounds. Change to Dark Navy, knit 2 rounds, purl 1 round, and knit 1¼ inches for the hem. Bind off.

FINISHING: Machine stitch and cut along the purl stitches for the waist edge and the boat neck openings (see Finishing, page

134). The neck opening is 11 ¾ inches wide, and will cut into the cable pattern on each side. Mark the neck opening by basting, then sew and cut. Using Dark Navy, pick up stitches along the neck, knit 2 rounds, purl 1 round, then knit 8 rounds increasing 2 stitches on each side of the neck every round.

Bind off and sew the hems to the purl side. Using Light Burgundy, pick up 220 stitches around the lower edge. Knit Border 1 in the round using the same colors as for the sleeves. Knit the border upside down to have the flowers in an upright position. Finish off by knitting 3 rounds of Light Burgundy, then change to Dark Navy and knit 2 rounds, purl 1 round, and knit 14 rounds for the hem. Bind off. Sew all the facings to the wrong side. Weave all loose ends into the back of the fabric. Steam lightly.

MODEL 20

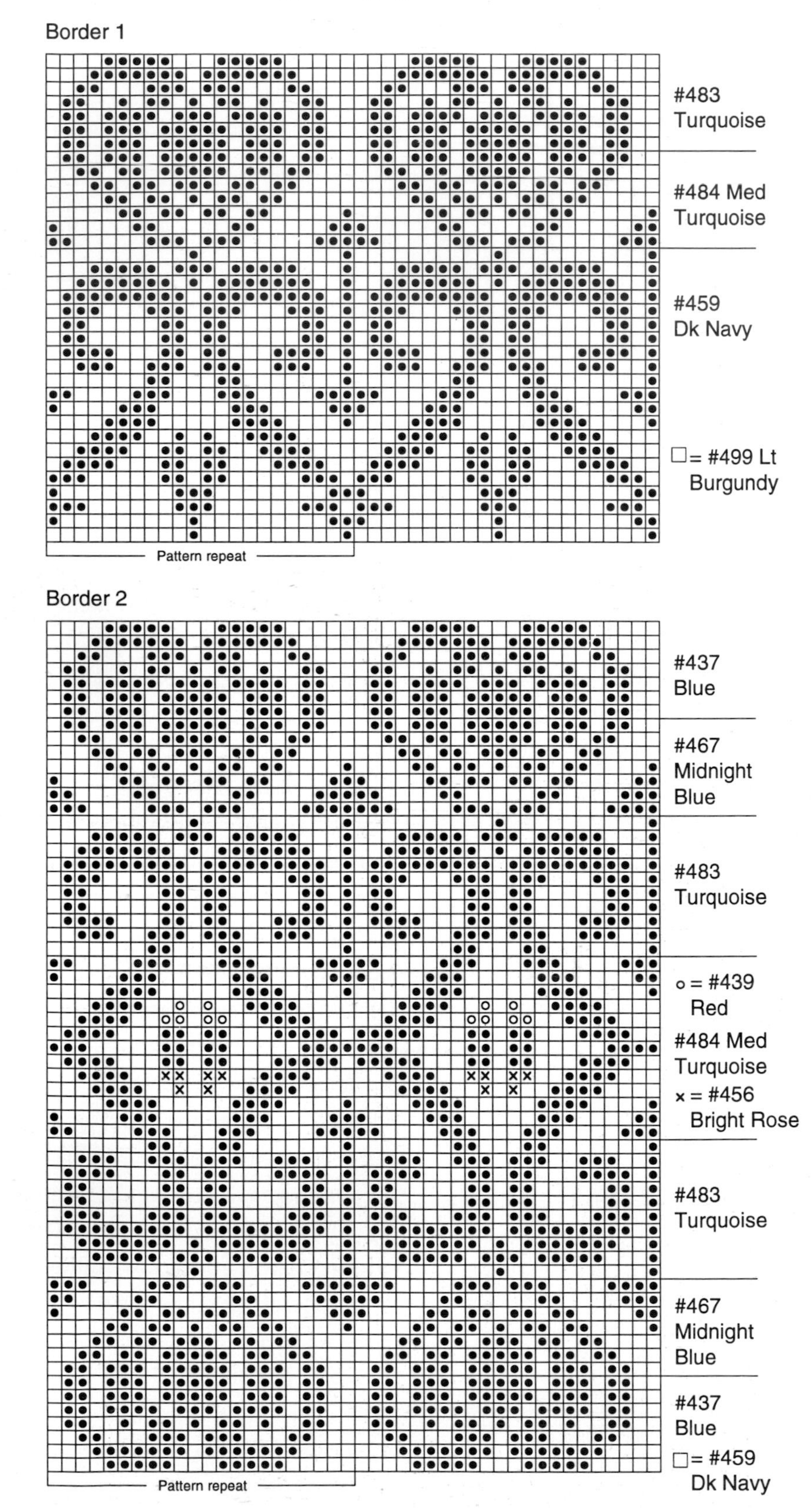

MODEL 21

"POOR MAN'S CHANEL" WITH GOLD BUTTONS

In the old days, people would knit star and flower designs using knit and purl stitches in an attempt to make them look like the rich people's damask fabrics. This kind of one-colored sweater was called "poor man's damask". This particular cardigan we have called "Poor Man's Chanel".

The thought behind this idea was to make a dressy cardigan using simple yarns. To make the whole cardigan with angora would cost hundreds of dollars just for the yarn.

Black wool for the cardigan and angora for the edgings would still be expensive. If the whole garment were made in only angora, we would probably not appreciate the beauty of the sweater.

Our idea was to make the soft angora be a gentle surprise when the cardigan was touched or looked at closely.

For the contrast in this design we have used mercerized cotton yarn. It looks like silk because it is so shiny. But it has the advantage of being washable, and, of course, it costs a lot less. The shiny cotton yarn in the sleeves makes the design stand out.

YARN: Rauma Istra and Symfoni

100% angora and metallic Gold threads along the edges.

Beads: Gold metallic beads

7 gold buttons

CHART: page 128

SIZES: S (M, L)

COLORS: #2036 Istra Black–300 (300, 350)g; #S18 Symfoni Blue–50 (50, 50)g; #S37 Symfoni DK Green–50 (50, 50)g; #S24 Symfoni Light Green–50 (50, 50)g; #S22 Symfoni Yellow–50 (50, 50)g; #S28 Symfoni Rose–50 (50, 50)g; #S12 Symfoni Black–350 (350, 350)g; Angora–20 (20, 20)g; Gold metallic–50 (50, 50)g

GAUGE: 22 stitches and 26 rounds = 4 × 4 inches

NEEDLE SUGGESTION: Circular and double-point knitting needles size 3mm and 3.5mm, or size necessary to obtain gauge. It is very important to knit to gauge otherwise the garment will be too big or too small.

CABLE PATTERN:

Rounds 1–5: *Knit 4 stitches, purl 2 stitches*, repeat between *'s around.

Round 6: *Slip the first 2 knit stitches onto a cable needle and hold to the front of the work, knit the next 2 stitches, knit the 2 stitches from the cable needle, purl 2 stitches*. Repeat between *'s around.

TRELLIS DESIGN: The "network" design is made by having groups of 2 stitches interchange place every other round. The design is set up as follows: *11 background stitches, 2 "network" stitches, 1 background stitch, 2 network stitches*, repeat between *'s. The "network" stitches move to each side, so the background on one side gets larger and the background on the other side gets smaller until the "network" stitches cross each other again. Work the "network" stitches like this: *To move to the right: Slip the stitch to the right of the 2 "network" stitches onto a cable needle and hold to the back of the work. Knit the 2 "network" stitches, then knit the stitch off the cable needle. Knit the background stitches. To move to the left: Slip the 2 "network" stitches onto a cable needle and hold to the front of the work, knit the next stitch, then knit the 2 stitches off the cable needle. Work the background stitches*. Repeat between *'s around. Knit 1 round between each round in which the stitches are moved. When you have 1 background stitch between the "network" stitches, cross the stitches as follows: *Slip the 2 "network" stitches plus the background stitch onto a cable needle and hold to the front of the work. Knit the next 2 "network" stitches, then the background stitch, and finally the last 2 "network" stitches. Knit 11 background stitches*. Repeat between *'s around. Knit 1 round before moving stitches again.

BODY: Using smaller circular needle and Black Istra, cast on 220 stitches. Knit in the round. The 3 center front stitches are purled all the time using a double strand whenever possible. They are to be machine stitched and cut open for the front opening later on. Knit 1¼ inches for the hem, purl 1 round, and knit 2 rounds. Change to Gold metallic and angora. Beginning with angora, work stripes alternating the two colors for 5 rounds. Using Black Istra, knit 2 rounds. Change to larger needles. The cardigan is tapered, and has increases on each side at the underarm. Place the design as follows: 3 flowers on each front and 6 flowers on the back. The increased stitches on the sides are worked into a stripe pattern, alternating 1 stitch each of the two colors. These increases are worked on each side of the vertical stripe pattern between flowers at the underarms. Work the pattern according to the graph. The increases take place between the flower design and the stripe design.

Increase 1 stitch between the front and the striped side, and 1 stitch on the other side of the stripes—between the stripes and the back. The new stitches are incorporated into the stripe design, so that the striped side panels get wider as you go. Increase 2 stitches on each side every 4th round (1 stitch on each side of the stripes for a total of 4 stitches increased) until you have 240 (248, 256) stitches. Work until the sweater measures 12½ (12½, 13½) inches. To shape for the armholes, bind off 3 stitches centered on each side. On the next round, cast on 2 stitches over the bound-off stitches. Purl these 2 stitches all the time using both strands of yarn. They are to be sewn and cut open later on. Continue working in the round. The armhole shaping takes place on each side of the 2 purl stitches. Decrease 1 stitch on each side of the purl stitches (4 stitches decreased in one round) until 8 stitches have been decreased on each side of the armhole and 206 (214, 222) stitches remain. Then decrease 1 stitch on each side every 3rd round until you have decreased a total of 13 stitches on each side and 154 (162, 170) stitches remain. Work even until the garment measures 17¾ (17¾, 18¼) inches. Now shape for front neck, and work back and forth. Bind off the 16 center front stitches. Then bind off 2 stitches at each neck edge every 3 rows 6 times and at the same time, after the 3rd decrease, bind off the 18 center back stitches, and finish each side separately.

Decrease 2 stitches on each side of back neck every other row 3 times for back neck shaping and continue front neck shaping. Complete the 3rd pattern repeat and bind off.

SLEEVES: Using smaller double-point needles and Black Istra, cast on 48 stitches. Knit in the round. Work the hem and the lower border as for the body. Change to larger needles and Black Symfoni, and increase to 54 stitches evenly spaced. Work cables for 6 inches ending on Round 6. Then work the trellis design. By placing the crosses in the trellis design right above the cables, you get a nice transition. You should get one trellis square for every other cable. To make a smooth transition, increase in a way so you get 11 stitches between every other cable, 2 stitches that will change place and form a "network", 1 new stitch, and 2 stitches to form a "network". Then 11 background stitches again. You will have 72 stitches total, including a 1-stitch vertical along the underarm, which is where you will increase.

Knit the trellis design, and at the same time increase 2 stitches (1 on each side of the vertical row), every other round until you have 118 stitches. Knit until the sleeve measures 15¾ (16¼, 16½) inches. Then bind off 3 stitches centered at the underarm.

Working back and forth, decrease 1 stitch on each side of the sleeve (1 at the beginning and 1 at the end of the row) every other row until you have 92 stitches left. Then work the trellis design even until the sleeve cap (from where you started working back and forth) is as long as the armhole shaping on the body. Now decrease for a gathered sleeve cap as follows: Work 3 together across for 3 rows, then bind off the remaining stitches.

FINISHING: Machine stitch and cut the front and armhole openings (see Finishing, page 134). Graft the shoulders. Sew the hem on the body. Using smaller needles and Black Istra, pick up 115 stitches along the front edges. On the left side, work stockinette stitch for 2 rows, 5 rows of stripes alternating 1 stitch gold and 1 stitch angora, and 2 more rows of Black Istra. Then 1 row reversed stockinette stitch for the fold, followed by 9 rows of stockinette stitch for the facing (the back of the band). Bind off. On the right side you will need to make buttonholes. Make the holes on the second row using Gold metallic and angora. A buttonhole goes over 5 stitches, with 15 stitches between each hole. Start at the lower edge of the band and make the first buttonhole 3 stitches from the edge. *Bind off 5 stitches for the first buttonhole, knit 15 stitches*, repeat between *'s across, and end with knit 9. On the next row, cast on 5 stitches over each buttonhole and continue as for the right side. When you get to the 3rd row of the band facing, make another row of buttonholes. Complete the band, and sew the band facings to the purl side. Using Gold metallic, sew buttonhole stitches through both layers around each buttonhole. Using Black Istra, pick up stitches around the neck, and make a neck band to match the front bands. Decrease 1 stitch at each shoulder every other row. On the 2nd row of the stripe pattern, make the last buttonhole over 5 stitches, placed 3 stitches from the edge on the right side. Work as the front bands through the reversed stockinette stitch row. Now increase 1 stitch at each shoulder every other row. Make another buttonhole on the 3rd row of the facing. Complete the facing, and bind off. Sew all the facings to the wrong side. Weave all loose ends into the back of the fabric. Steam lightly. Sew on gold buttons, and sew gold beads on the trellis design on the sleeves.

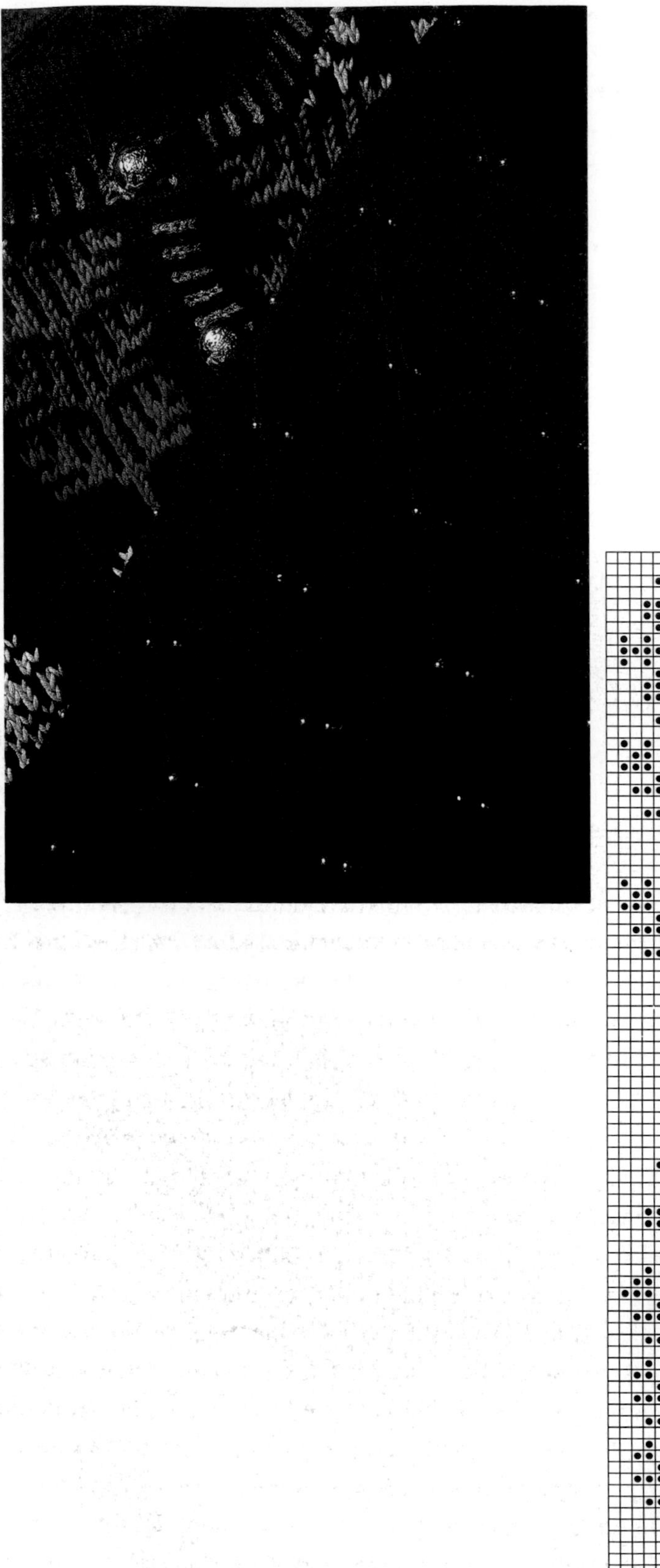

MODEL 21

#S28 Pink

#S22 Gold

#S24 Olive Green

#S37 Grey Green

#S18 Blue

#S28 Pink

#S22 Gold

#S24 Olive Green

#S37 Grey Green

#S18 Blue

□ = #2036 Black Istra

End

Pattern repeat

MAKING CABLE AND TRELLIS DESIGNS

The sleeve design on Model 21 consists of cables and trellis. The patterns for this type of design can look terribly complicated, but, in fact, they are not. They are logically built up and our advise is: Don't use a pattern; use your head instead!

Cables

To make cables, you'll need a cable needle, which you can buy in a yarn shop, in addition to circular or double-pointed needles. The cable needle is shorter than other needles, and the curved center part prevents the stitches from falling off too easily. Because they are shorter, cable needles are more comfortable to use than regular needles, which tend to get in the way when making cables. The main thing to remember about cable knitting is that the stitches change position on the needle in a certain order. Usually, you knit at least one round between rounds in which the stitches change position.

Following is a description of two simple cables you can make. When you understand the principle of cable knitting, you'll be able to create your own variations. Using three double-point needles and sport or worsted weight yarn, cast on 36 stitches (12 stitches on each needle). Knit 3 rounds or make a short ribbing to prevent the swatch from curling. *Purl 2, knit 4 for 4 rounds. Then purl 2 and slip the next 2 stitches onto the cable needle without knitting them and hold them to the front of the work while knitting the next 2 stitches. Put the cable needle parallel to the left-hand needle and knit the 2 stitches off the cable needle. You have now made your first cable. Purl 2 stitches and make another cable over the 4 next knit stitches. Repeat as described around, then purl 2, and knit 4 for 8 rounds.* Make cables on the next round and repeat between *s until you are comfortable with this technique.

Now it is time for further experimentation. How would it look, for example, if only 2 stitches changed place? Or 4? Model 15 has a design where only 2 stitches change position. The number of rounds worked between each cable round will also change the look of the design. How would it look to work stockinette or maybe moss stitch between the cables instead of purl stitches? Could the areas between the cables be worked in another color? And what happens if you hold the stitches on the cable needle to the back of the work instead of to the front? In other words, cables can be worked in many ways.

Trellis

A "bashful" blue swatch gave us the idea for the sleeves for the "Poor Man's Channel". The original plan was to make a blue cotton sweater with cables instead of ribbing. We were thinking of a trellis design with flower embroidery. However, the blue cotton sweater was never made, but with a few adjustments, the swatch became useful after all. The trellis consists mostly of plain knitted surfaces, while the cables are quite tight and pull together, making a nice contrast to gathered sleeve caps.

The main thing to remember about making a trellis design is that 2 stitches move one stitch over to the right, and 2 stitches move one stitch over to the left every 2nd or 3rd round. Between the moved stitches, you create stockinette-stitched diamonds.

To make a simple trellis design, use a relatively heavy yarn, cast on 56 stitches, and distribute them over 4 double-point needles (14 stitches on each needle). Knit a few rounds or work up a short ribbing. On the next round, *knit 5 and place a piece of yarn as a marker around the next 4 stitches as you knit them*. Repeat between *'s around.

On the next round, knit 4 stitches, slip the next stitch onto the cable needle and hold it to the back of the work, knit 2 marked stitches, and then knit the stitch from the cable needle. Slip the next 2 marked stitches onto the cable needle and hold them to the front of the work, knit the next stitch, then knit the 2 stitches from the cable needle. Repeat this around. Now knit 1 round. On the next round, knit the 3 first stitches before slipping 1 onto the cable needle. Always knit 1 round between each round of moving stitches.

As you continue, you will have more and more stitches inside the diamond and less and less outside it. When all the stitches are finally inside the diamond, the 4 stitches forming the trellis will be next to each other. They have to change place now, like cables. Slip 2 stitches onto the cable needle and hold to the front of the work, knit 1, and then knit the last 2 and the stitches inside the diamond. Slip the last stitch before the next 2 trellis stitches onto the cable needle and hold to the back of the work, knit the 2 trellis stitches, and then knit the stitch from the cable needle. Repeat around.

What possibilities do you have with a trellis design? You can do some embroidery inside the diamonds, sew beads on each intersection, or do a different stitch inside the diamonds. You can also elaborate a little at each intersection by making some cables before you go on to the next diamond. Or you can make the diamonds smaller or larger. Or, if you knit more than one round between moving rounds, the diamonds will be more pointed. You can also use more than two stitches to form the trellis, or only one.

PART IV
METHODS

KNITTING TECHNIQUES

Shaping a garment is not as difficult as you may think. If you can cast on, increase, and decrease, you have the basics needed to make any kind of garment. In this section we will describe these basic techniques.

CASTING ON: (1) The most common method is the long-tail cast-on. To begin this method, figure out how long a tail you need to cast on by measuring from the tip of your index finger to your wrist. You'll get approximately 10 stitches out of this length. Measure this length repeatedly, counting by tens until you have enough yarn for the number of stitches you want to cast on. Next, make a slip-knot and place it on a knitting needle. Then put the tail end around your left thumb and the other end around your left index finger. A loop now sits between your thumb and index finger. Hold both tails together with your other left hand fingers. With the needle in your right hand, bring it to the left side of your thumb and into the loop that forms around your thumb. Bring the tip of the needle towards the tip of your left index finger, pick up that strand and pull it through the thumb loop, and then slide this loop off your thumb. Repeat until you have enough stitches.

(2) If you need a more elastic cast-on edge, perhaps for a hat, try using the following method: Make a slip-knot and place it on your knitting needle. (You do not need a long tail for this method). With a second

LONG-TAIL CAST-ON

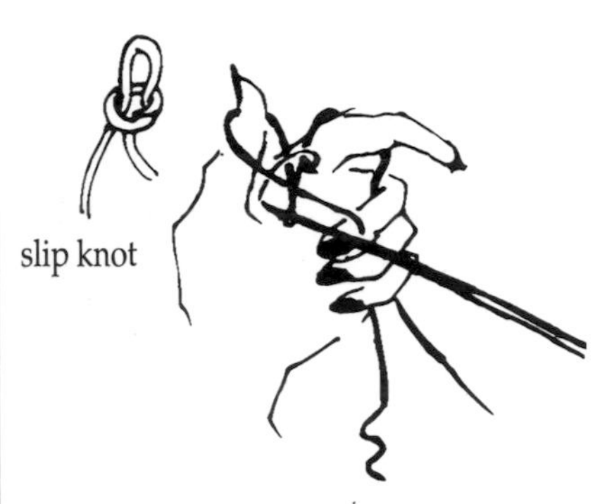

1. Make a slip knot around the needle, hold the yarn as shown, and take the needle up through the thumb loop, around the yarn on the left side of the index finger, and back through the thumb loop.

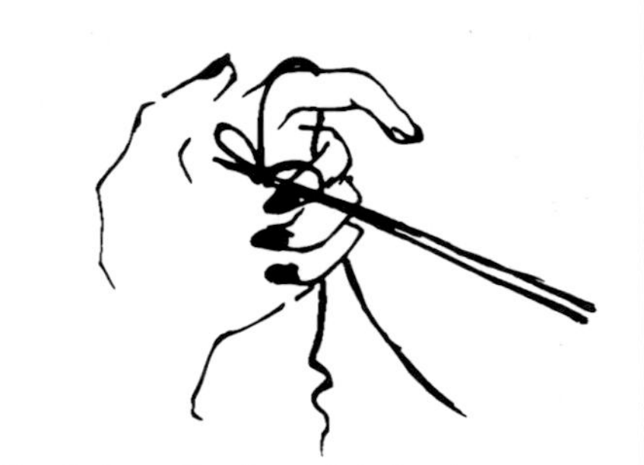

2. Let the loop slip off your left thumb.

3. Pull up the stitch as you pick up the tail again onto your left thumb.

needle, knit a new stitch through the loop and put the stitch on the needle with the loop. Then knit a new stitch through the last stitch made and slip it on to the left-hand needle. Repeat until you have enough stitches.

INCREASING: There is a horizontal strand between two knitted stitches. To increase, place your needle under this strand from the back and then knit it. When a pattern instructs you to increase two stitches under the sleeve (the "seam"), it looks best if you knit one or two stitches between increases.

DECREASING: The simplest decrease is to knit 2 stitches together. Another decrease method is to slip one stitch without knitting it, knit the next stitch, and then pass the slipped stitch over the knit stitch. This method will slant the stitch in the opposite direction than the previous method of knitting two stitches together. Experiment to find out which method works best for you.

CASTING OFF: To cast off all stitches, for instance, at the top of a sleeve, do as follows: Knit 2 stitches and pass the first stitch (the one to the right side) over the second. Then knit a third stitch, and pass it over the second. Continue this way until you have one stitch left on your needle. Break the yarn and pull the tail through the last stitch.

KNITTING THROUGH THE BACK LOOP: Each stitch you knit is actually a piece of yarn hanging over a needle. By making a knit stitch, you pull the yarn through the loop on the needle, going into the loop from left to right. If you go into the loop from right to left, you knit through the back loop, making a twisted stitch.

PURLING THROUGH THE BACK LOOP: With the yarn in front of the needle, go behind the loop and into it from left to right and pick up the strand from the front.

Purling through the back loop: Insert the right needle into the stitch from behind, then follow the arrow with the needle point.

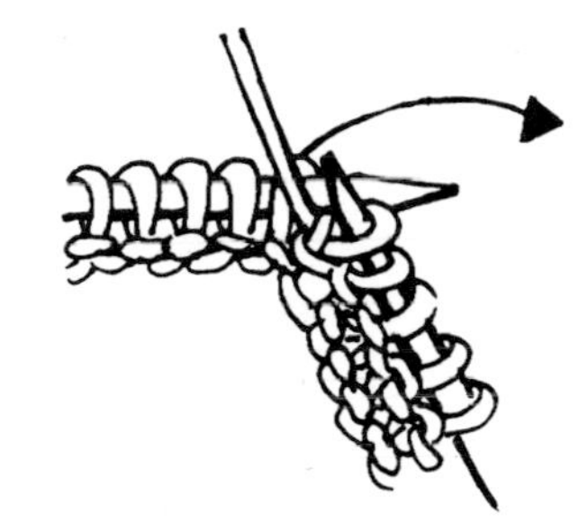

Slip the stitch off the left needle.

WEAVING IN THE LOOSE ENDS: You can weave in the loose ends by using a yarn needle when you have finished your knitting. You can also weave in the ends as you knit. If you choose the latter method and knit continental style (called "picking"), keep the working yarn to the right on your left index finger and the tail end to the left (closer to your knuckle). Knit by going alternately over and under the short end. Repeat this five or six times to fasten the tail. Before you cut off the end, pull that row of your knitting a little sideways.

If you knit the American way (called "throwing"), you flip the tail ends alternately over and under the yarn. Then finish off in the same manner described above. You can use these same techniques to avoid long loops on the back when working a two-color design with more than seven consecutive stitches in the same color.

GRAFTING/KITCHENER STITCH: This technique allows you to sew shoulders together without casting off the stitches first. This gives a more elastic seam. Sew with yarn, using an appropriate color. Leave the stitches on two needles and place the needles in a parallel position. Sew through one stitch from one needle and then one stitch from the other needle. The result should look like a knitted row, as the drawing illustrates.

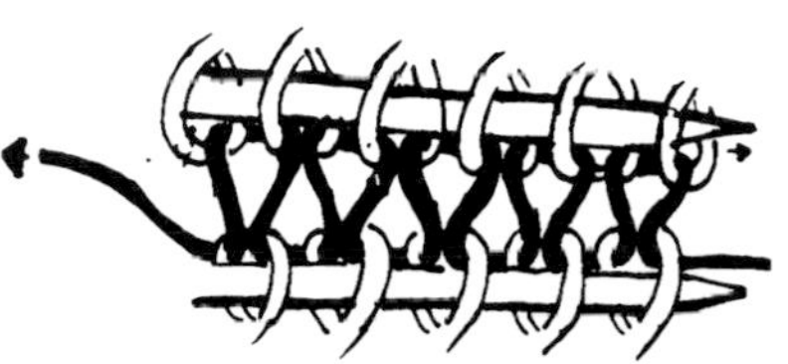

Kitchner stitch: Sew through one stitch from one needle and then one stitch from the other needle as shown.

You can also knit the shoulders together from the purl side. To do so, place the needles in a parallel position, and then use a third knitting needle to knit 2 stitches together—one stitch from each needle. When you have all the stitches on one needle, cast them off as described under "Casting off", page 132.

CHARTED PATTERNS: On a chart, the main color is usually shown as an open square, and the contrast color as a dark circle or other symbol. In reading the pattern directions, you will often run across the word repeat. One repeat is the smallest unit in a design. Usually, the same repeat is repeated several times—back and forth or up and down—to form a design. Sometimes the repeats do not come out even with the number of stitches you have. If this happens on the body, you should stop knitting the design and knit one or more stitches—called marking stitches—on the sides using the darkest color in the design. On the sleeve, it might look best to knit one or more marking stitches under the sleeve (as a "seam"). The increase will then take place on each side of the "seam" stitches.

To get a nice, even look, make sure you are consistent in the way you carry the different colors. If you are doing a design where you knit the same number of stitches in each of two colors, like vertical stripes, it is even more important to be consistent.

DUPLICATE STITCHING: Duplicate stitching is a recommended knitting technique when you are using more than two colors and have many strands to keep track of or if there are many stitches in one color before a stitch in one of the other colors. The duplicate stitch is an embroidery stitch that is done after you finish your knitting. This stitch looks like a knitted stitch, forming Vs stacked inside one another. To make this stitch, come up to the knit side at the point—the base of the V—of a stitch, go behind the stitch in the next row up, and go back to the purl side at the point where you started. Repeat as necessary from right to left.

Duplicate stitching gives you many decorative possibilities that regular two-color knitting does not. You can, for example, base your design on an idea from a cross-stitch pattern. If you are doing a large area in duplicate stitch, it looks best to use a slightly thinner yarn than you used in your knitting.

BUTTONHOLES: Buttonholes can be made in different ways. The most common way is to cast off a certain number of stitches in one row and then cast on the same number of stitches in the next row. You can also slip the buttonhole stitches onto a piece of scrap yarn. When you finish knitting, pull out the scrap piece and use a yarn needle to run your yarn through the buttonhole stitches and couple times. To finish off, sew buttonhole stitches all the way around the buttonhole.

NECK OPENINGS: Many patterns require you to cast off stitches for the front and the back neck openings and continue to work the garment until the body reaches full length. You can do this in two different ways: 1. After you have cast off the front neck stitches, you must maintain the design by working back and forth until you reach the length where you cast off for the back neck. From this point, you must finish the right and the left side separately. 2. This method allows you to knit in the round all the way up. To begin, cast off for the front neck as described in the above paragraph. On the next round, cast on 3 new stitches over the cast-off stitches. Then purl all the new stitches, working them in a double strand (main plus contrast color). This strengthens for cutting and machine stitching. Now cast off for the back neck opening, and repeat the procedure. After finishing the body, sew two machine seams on each side of the center purl stitch and cut open between the machine seams. Finally, pick up the appropriate number of stitches around the neck opening and work the ribbing or facing as indicated in your pattern. You can use this same technique for other places where you need an opening but prefer to knit in the round.

FACINGS/HEMS: A hem is often used to finish off the body or the sleeves instead of ribbing. At the top of the sleeves and around the neck, a facing is needed to cover up the cut edge. Start the sleeve facing by purling one round. This marks the beginning of the facing and gives you one round to sew into when sewing in the sleeve. Whenever you have to purl a complete round, you can simply turn your work inside out and knit around instead. Then turn it right side out again and finish the facing.

When knitting a facing for a square neck, you must increase one stitch at each corner every round to make the facing lay flat when you turn it to the inside. If you make facings for a square corner, like the lower front corner of a cardigan, you must decrease rather than increase to obtain the right shape.

FINISHING: In most patterns, the body and the sleeves are knitted separately in the round, and the sleeves are sewn to the body when finishing. To finish your garment, mark the sides of the body and measure the width of the sleeve. Use this measurement to mark the distance from the shoulder edges of the body down to the appropriate points along the sides. You may want to baste the sleeve opening. Sew a machine seam along one stitch down to the marker, across one stitch (and your basting), and up on the other side to the shoulder. Sew another machine seam close to the first one for safety. Use a 3-stitch zigzag, if your machine has that option. If not, use a regular straight seam and short stitches. Make sure the sweater does not stretch too much lengthwise when sewing. If you are making a cardigan, machine stitch two seams on each side of the center front. Then cut open between the machine seams and graft or knit the shoulders together as described on page 133.

After you've finished the sleeve seams, put the sleeves to the body with right sides together, and sew the sleeves in by hand using yarn. Sew just inside the cast-off round or in the purl round if you made a facing. On the body, sew the side seams together just inside the machine seams. If you made a facing, fold it over the cut edge and slip stitch it to the body. Sew other facings or hems to the purl side. Work the neck according to the pattern. Weave in all the tails and steam your work lightly under a damp cloth. Some people feel that knitwear should not be steamed, but that is a matter of opinion.

Through the years, many books have been written about knitting techniques. It is an extensive subject—there are so many ways to cast on, cast off, increase, and decrease. We covered only the techniques you'll need in order to finish the patterns in this book.

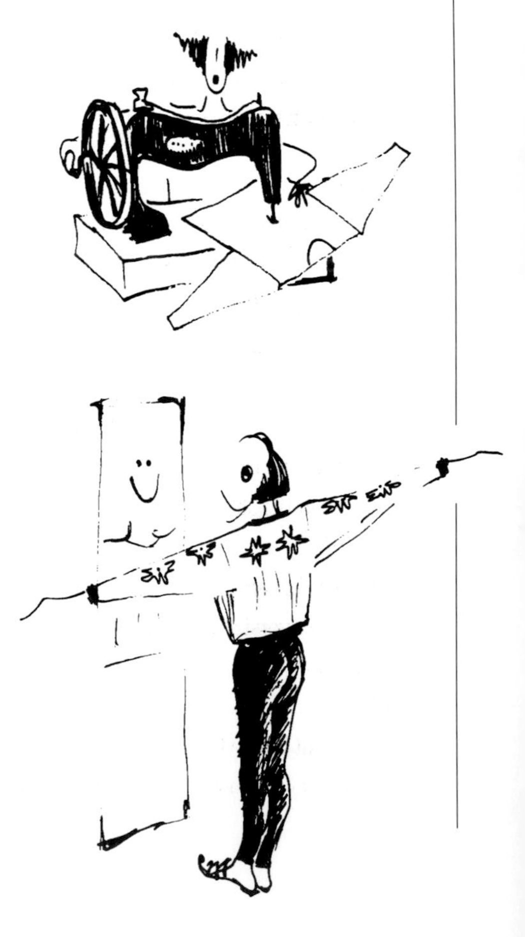

MAKING YOUR OWN PATTERNS

Swatches and Gauges

Before you start kniting a garment, make a swatch of the design you plan to knit. Make several swatches if you aren't sure how tight or loose you should knit. Feel the swatch with your hands. It should not be so tight that the garment will feel stiff to wear or so loose that it looks sloppy. Most yarn has a suggested gauge printed on the label. Use this gauge as a guide, but remember that you may have to use one size larger needles to obtain the given gauge when knitting a design in several colors. If you work with one color, try the given needle size.

Basic Sweater

When you plan a basic pattern on paper, start with the measurements in the table in this book (page 136) or measure your favorite sweater. Draw the outline of the garment or make a tissue paper model based on the given measurements for our basic pattern. Measure around the hips and the bust and from the shoulder down for the body length.

Our sweaters are not tightly fitted. They are relatively oversized, and if you want them more fitted adjust your paper pattern accordingly.

To find out if the sleeves will fit, you'll need to do more than just measure the sleeve from the body to the wrist and compare with your body measurement from shoulder to wrist. Since the sweater is oversized, you will have a drop shoulder. Therefore, you must measure the length from the wrist and over the shoulders to the other wrist, with slightly bent arms. Compare this measurement with the length from wrist to wrist on the paper pattern. If you make the body narrower, the sleeves need to be longer, and if the body is wider, the sleeves need to be shorter.

When you have adjusted the pattern to the size you want, draw the lines with a marker. Put tissue paper over your drawing and cut out several "garments". You can use the extra paper patterns to further plan your garment. Think about how to place borders, what colors to use, what kind of edgings you want, et cetera, and take careful notes. The first time you plan your own pattern, it might be a good idea to copy your various designs and paste them directly on to your outline.

Basic Patterns

Before designing a garment, you should make a basic pattern that can be used for many garments. On page 137, you will learn how to adjust this basic pattern to a specific sweater you want to make.

Let us pretend you need to determine how many stitches to cast on for the sleeve. From your swatch, you know how many stitches it takes to knit 4 inches × 4 inches. For instance, if your gauge is 28 stitches and 32 rounds over 4 inches × 4 inches, this means that you have 7 stitches to one inch (28 ÷ 4=7), and 8 rounds to one inch (32 ÷ 4=8).

The table on page 136 gives the measurements for the length and width of all the sizes. For example, in the "cuff circumference" measurement column you will find how wide the sleeve cuff for your size should be. Multiply this number by 7 and round it off to a whole number. This tells you how many stitches you will need to cast on for the sleeves.

To find out how many rounds to knit for the sleeves, find the meassurement for "total sleeve length" in the table, and multiply this by 8. Then round this number off to a whole number.

Now determine the gauge of the yarn you want to use. Copy the pattern below inserting your own numbers. The different measurements for width and length are written in parentheses and need to be substituted with the standard measurements for your size in the table on page 136. Multiply the standard measurement (indicated with an x) by the number of stitches per inch (sts/inch) or by the number of rounds per inch (rds/inch).

THE BODY: Cast on (hip circumference × sts/inch) stitches and work the ribbing, hem, or facing for the number of inches needed for a particular size, or for the length you prefer. Increase evenly until you have (circumference above hips × sts/inch). For boat neck, work (total length × rds/inch) rounds. Cast off. Sew the shoulders, leaving a comfortable opening for the neck.

MEASUREMENTS FOR STANDARD SIZES

Sizes	1/2	1	2	3	6	9	12	S	M	L	XL	XXL
THE SLEEVE												
cuff circumference	4¼	4¾	4¾	5½	5¼	6	6¼	7	7½	8	8¼	8¾
ribbing or hem	1¼	1¼	1¼	1¼	2	2	2	2	2	2	2	2
circumference above cuff	6½	6½	8	8	8¾	9½	9½	9½	10	10¾	10¾	13
length above cuff*	5½	7½	8¾	9½	12	13¾	16½	19	18½	18¼	17¾	17¼
total sleeve length*	6¾	8¾	10	10¾	13¾	15¾	18½	21	20½	20	19¾	19¼
circumference at top of sleeve	12½	13¾	15¾	17¼	18½	20½	23	23	25¼	26¾	30	31¼
THE BODY												
hip circumference	19	20½	22	23	25¼	28	31½	35½	39½	41¾	43¼	47¼
ribbing or hem	1¼	1¼	1¼	2	2	2	2	2	2	2	2	
circumference above ribbing	20½	23¾	26¾	28¼	30	33	37	41¾	44	47¼	52	56
length in front to square neck	8¼	9½	11	12	13¾	15¾	18½	21¼	21¾	22½	23	23¾
width of cast-off at square neck	3¼	3½	4	4	4	4¼	4¾	5½	5½	5½	6¼	6¼
length in back to square neck	9¾	11¼	12½	13¼	15½	17¾	20½	23	23½	24	24¾	25½
total length	10¼	11¾	13	13¾	16	18¼	21	24	24¾	25½	26¼	26¾

*Note: because the instructions are written for drop-shoulder shapings, the sleeve lengths for the larger adult sizes are shorter that the sleeve lengths for the smaller adult sizes.

For a square neck, work (length in front to square neck × rds/inch) rounds. Cast off (width of cast-off for square neck × sts/inch) stitches at center front. Continue working until the garment measures (length in back for square neck) inches at center back. Cast off (width of cast-off at square neck × sts/inch) stitches at center back. Work until the garment measures (total length) inches. Put the stitches on holders.

THE SLEEVES: Cast on (cuff circummference x sts/inch) stitches and work the ribbing, hem, or facing for given number of inches for a particular size, or desired length. Increase evenly to (circumference above cuff x sts/inch). Now increase 2 stitches under the sleeve every so often until the sleeve reaches full length. To figure out how often you need to increase, compute (circumference at top of sleeve × sts/inch) stitches minus (circumference above cuff × sts/inch) and divide the resulting number by 2. Then divide (length above cuff × rds/inch) rounds by the last number you figured and round it off to a whole number. If the number is 3, you will increase 2 stitches every 3rd round. An increase every 3rd or 4th round—or every other round for very full sleeves—seems to work well. Increases 2 stitches every (whatever round you determine) round until the sleeve meassures (total sleeve length) desired number of inches, or until you have worked (length above cuff × rds/inch) rounds. Purl 1 round and then knit for approximately 3/4" for the facing. Skip the facing if you are working with a bulky yarn. Cast off and work the other sleeve to match.

FINISHING: Measure the upper edge of the sleeve to determine how large a sleeve opening you need to cut on the body. Place marker, sew two machine seams, and cut open. (The Knitting Technique section explains more in detail on how to finish the garment). Weave in all the tails and sew any facings to the purl side. You may want to refer to one of the patterns if you have questions about any of these techniques.

Adjustments to the Basic Pattern

Once you have written a pattern using your own measurements, you have created your own basic pattern. Using this basic pattern, you can now make a pattern for that specific garment you have in mind. If your design does not come out even with the number of stitches in your basic pattern you can adjust that in two different ways. One way is to round up, so the design comes out even with the number of stitches you need to complete your repeats. Correspondingly, you can round off the number of rounds—up or down—so you come out even both around and length wise. This is the most practical approach if you are using the same design all over the garment and are working with relatively small repeats.

Another way to adjust is to use side marking "seam" stitches. These marking stitches are always worked in the darkest color of the pattern. First, stop working the design on the sides of the body (or under the sleeve). If your repeat consists of an uneven number of stitches, subtract 6 from the number of stitches on the body after the ribbing and round off to a number divisible by 4 (of the 6 stitches you subtracted, 2 are marking stitches on each side plus 1 stitch at the center front and 1 stitch at the center back). On the sleeve, subtract 3 stitches after finishing the ribbing and round off to a number divisible by 2 (of the 3 stitches you subtracted, 2 are marking stitches under the sleeve plus 1 stitch at the center of the sleeve). Mark the center front and center back stitch on the body plus 2 stitches on each side. Now make sure that the center stitch for your repeat matches the center front and the center back stitch. Count from the center stitch to the side marking stitches. (If you do not count the 6 marking stitches, the number of stitches for one side should be one-quarter of the total stitch number. Also, the center of the repeat on the sleeve should match the center sleeve stitch).

If the number of stitches is an even number, subtract 4 from the number of stitches after the ribbing and round it off to a number divisible by 4 (the 4 stitches you subtract are the side-marking stitches). In this case, the two repeats will meet at the center front and center back. Subtract 2 stitches on the sleeve from the number of stitches after the ribbing. Here, the two repeats will meet at the center of the sleeve.

You can, of course, use only one marking stitch on each side, as done for the models in this book. On the body, subtract 4 stitches if you have a repeat with an uneven number, and 2 stitches if your repeat has an even number. For the sleeves, subtract accordingly 1 and 2 stitches. That way, the design on each side of the increases will be symmetrical.

On your drawing, mark the center front

and the center back, and with an arrow, show where in the repeat you need to start after you knit the "seam" stitches. Do the same for the sleeves. The stitches under the sleeve are marking stitches. Mark the center sleeve stitch and count where in the repeat you will start after you knit the "seam" stitches. The sleeve increases occur on each side of the "seam" stitches.

Write a Pattern

Now try to write a pattern that is clear enough for even other people to follow. If you think this exercise is difficult, you can use another pattern as a model. As you knit, write down any changes. When the garment is done, write out a copy to keep in a binder together with your drawing. There are many good reasons for having a binder for your own patterns. When you want to make another pattern, you can refer to one of your older ones to avoid making the same mistake twice. If others like your sweater, you may want to loan them your pattern. And if your pattern is really good, you can even try to sell it to a magazine or yarn company. Congratulations, you have become your own knitwear designer!

EXPERIMENT WITH DIFFERENT SHAPES

So far, you have learned to create a design for a drop shoulder garment, where the sleeves increase evenly all the way to the shoulder. The body can either be knit straight up to the neck shaping after the increases following the ribbing, or it can have increases evenly spaced along the sides to make it more tapered. When you have learned this, you can knit anything with straight lines. But who says a garment has to look like A? B shows some of the other possible shapes.

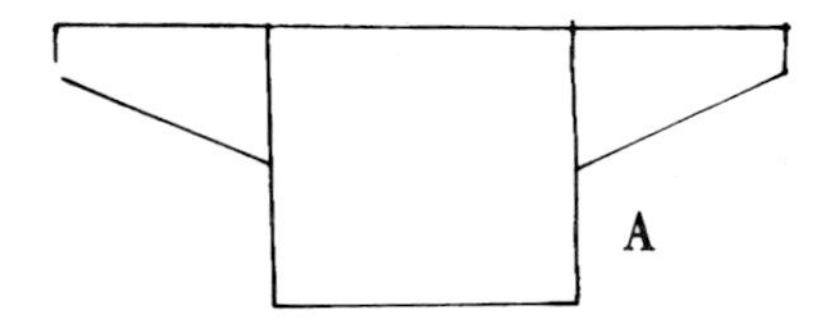

It is always a good idea to draw the garment in its actual size on a piece of paper. Then you can write down all the measurements you will need in order to figure out the different increases. To make a sleeve as in C, you need to calculate the same way you did when you were figuring out the increases for the regular sleeve in your basic pattern. Measure width 2 and width 1 and find out how many stitches you need for each width. The difference between the two measurements or number of stitches is

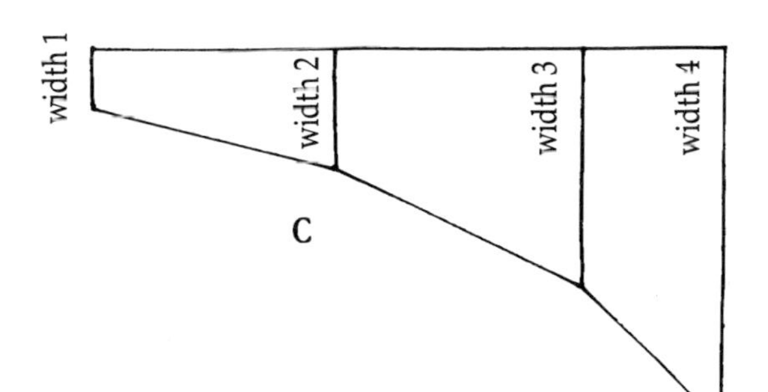

B

equivalent to how many stitches you need to increase. If you increase two stitches at a time, divide the number by two. Increase evenly over the number of rounds you need to knit. (Measure the length and convert into rounds). By dividing the number of rounds by the number of increases, you get the number that tells you how often you need to increase. This number is not always an even number, so you have to adjust it either up or down. For example, if the number is 2.3, you will increase alternately every 2nd round. If the number is 2.5, you will increase alternately every 2nd and 3rd round. If the number is 2.7, you will increase every 3rd round. Figure out all the different increases like this, and you will get a sleeve looking like the one in C.

Curves

A knitted garment does not have to be "square" or formed by straight lines. Imagine that a curved line is made up of many short straight lines. A knitted curve is composed of many increases. With curves, you can knit just about anything (D). Divide the curve into small sections and find out where it changes character. Figure out all the different increases separately and combine them to make a pattern (E).

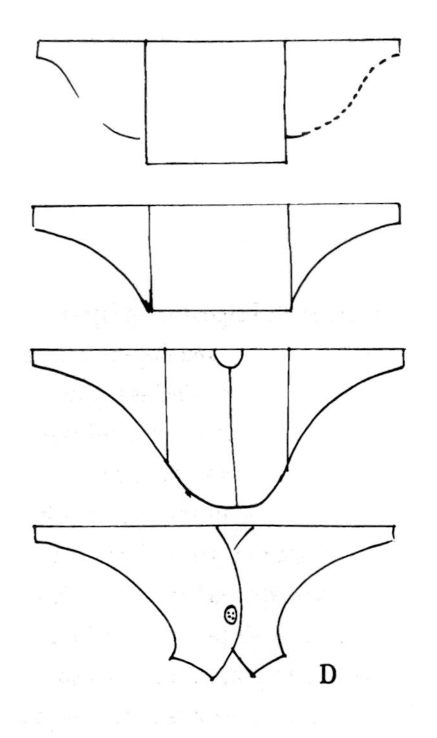

Curves and slanted lines in knitting are created the same way. When you increase at certain given places, like on the sides of a body or under a sleeve as seen in the sketches so far, you get a "flat garment". If you put them down on the floor, they are flat, just as if you would lay down on the floor yourself and have someone draw your contour.

By using the following principles, you can make a more fully shaped garment. You can make a set-in sleeve with a shaped sleeve cap (F), or you can spread the increases more evenly around the garment, just like you do after knitting the ribbing (G). If you increase or decrease a lot in one round, you can create ruffles (H).

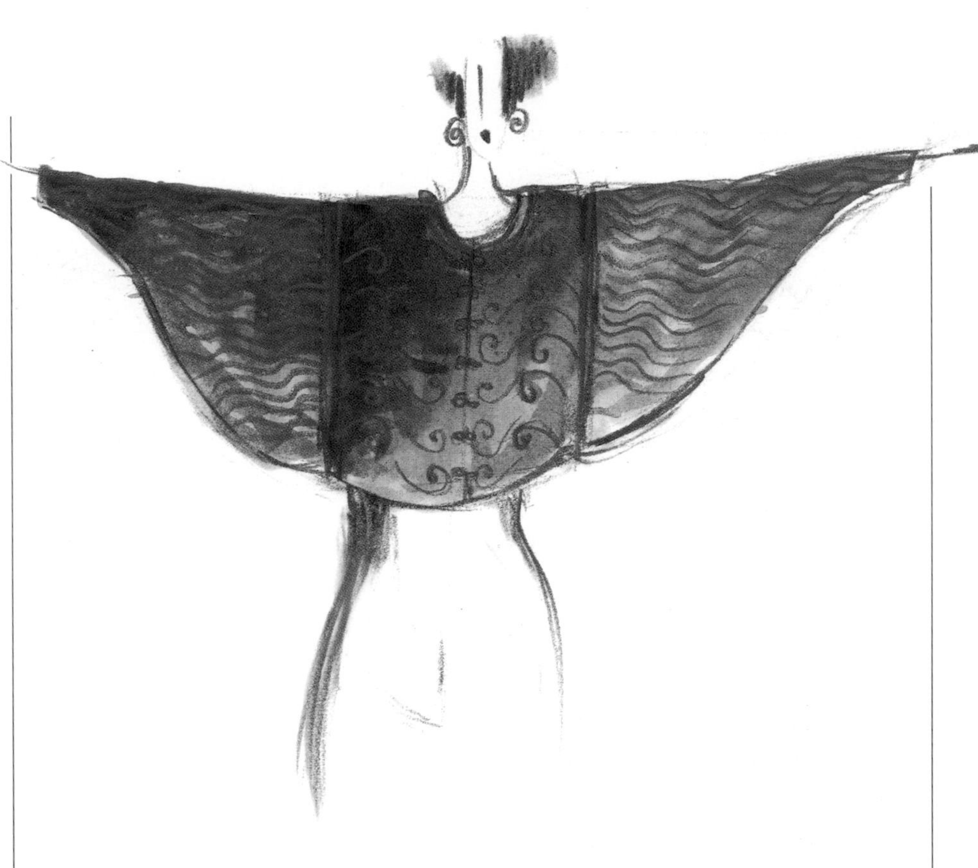

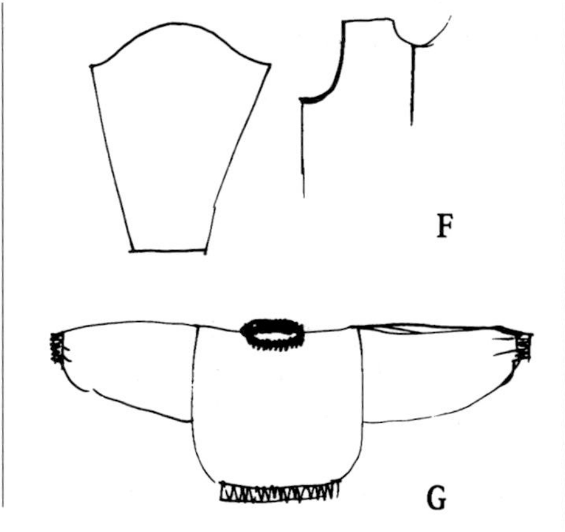

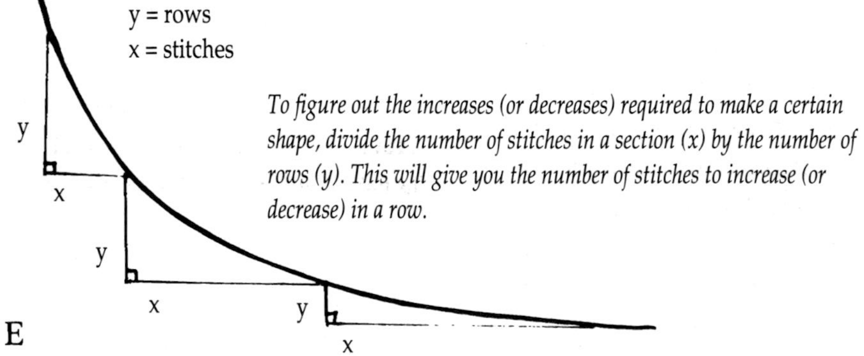

To figure out the increases (or decreases) required to make a certain shape, divide the number of stitches in a section (x) by the number of rows (y). This will give you the number of stitches to increase (or decrease) in a row.

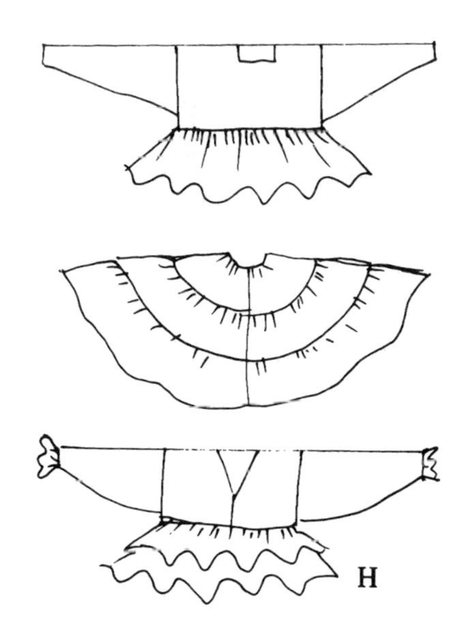

(I) is an example of a round yoke, where decreases are evenly distributed around the garment. The shape of the sweater is determined by how often you increase and decrease in one round, and how many rounds you knit between each increase or decrease. You can make a narrow funnel or a flat round shape following the same principles (J). The top of a pill box hat is an example of the latter.

To make a flat round shape, you need to vary the number of stitches between each time you increase/decrease and also the number of rounds you knit between increases/decreases. Start a sample as follows: Cast on 4 stitches. *Knit 1 stitch, increase 1*, repeat between *s around. Knit 1 round without increases. Next round: *Knit 2, increase 1*, repeat between *s around. Knit 2 rounds without increases. Next round: *Knit 3, increase 1*, repeat between *s around. Knit 3 rounds without increases. Continue like this until your round shape is the desired size.

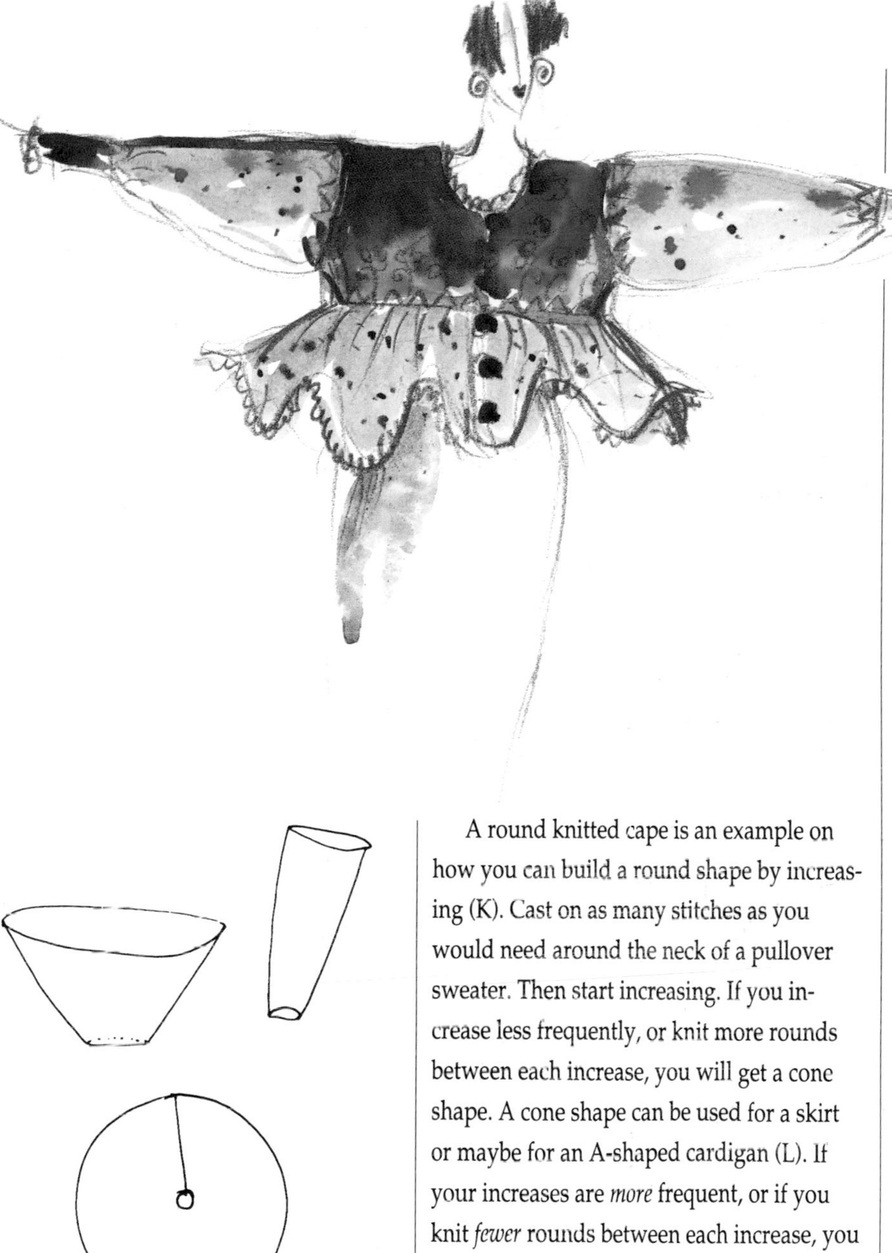

J

If you want to work from the outside in, reverse the pattern and decrease where you increased. The number of stitches decreased— and number of rounds between each decrease—will gradually be reduced.

A round knitted cape is an example on how you can build a round shape by increasing (K). Cast on as many stitches as you would need around the neck of a pullover sweater. Then start increasing. If you increase less frequently, or knit more rounds between each increase, you will get a cone shape. A cone shape can be used for a skirt or maybe for an A-shaped cardigan (L). If your increases are *more* frequent, or if you knit *fewer* rounds between each increase, you can make ruffles (M).

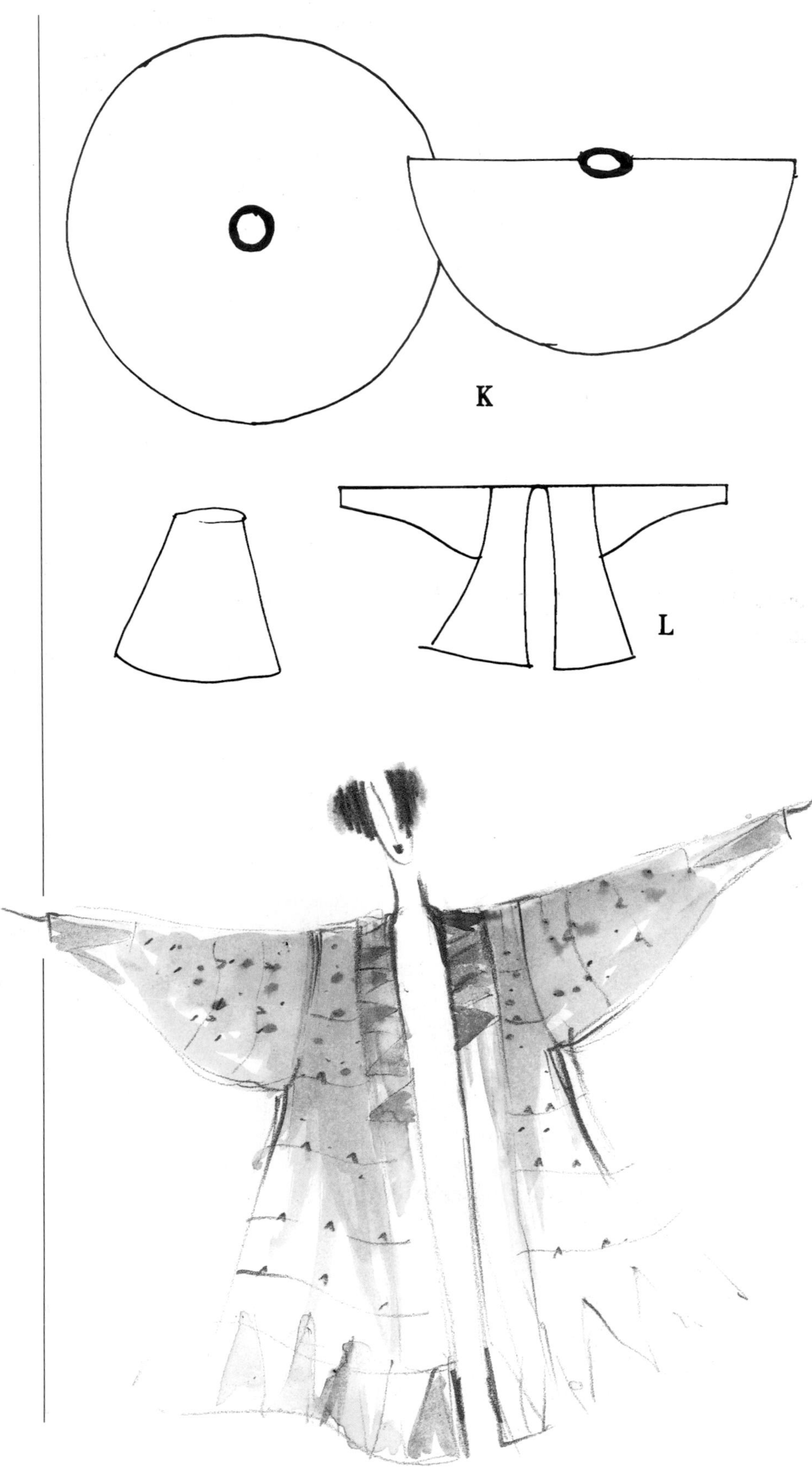

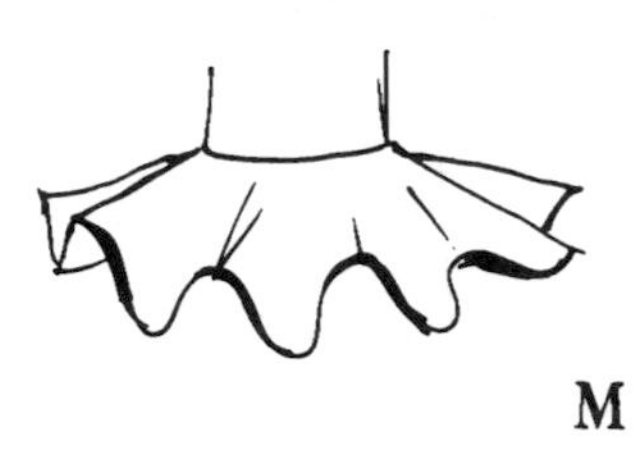

Another way of shaping is to make gussets. Model 16 in this book is made that way. It is built up with many gussets that become more narrow as you approach the neck. The shape of such a garment is determined by the number of gussets, and how often you increase/decrease (N). You can also incorporate a gusset into a design by making the garment follow the shape of the gusset.

A gusset is shaped as a sleeve is, by increasing/decreasing along straight lines (O). To determine how often you need to increase, you must figure out the difference between the number of stitches at the lower edge (A) and the upper edge (B) of the gusset. Divide the difference between A and B by 2, so you can increase 1 stitch on each side of the gusset. By measuring the length of the gusset, you will know how many rounds you have for your increases and can then figure out an even distribution.

It takes a little practice to see how a shape looks in a "flat" condition, that is, how each part of a garment would look if you cut it into pieces and laid each piece out on the floor. It is necessary to be able to visualize and draw each piece "flat" to work out the increases/decreases. Start with a garment you already have. Draw it out flat in actual size on a piece of paper, and then try to see how you can transfer the shape into a knitting pattern.

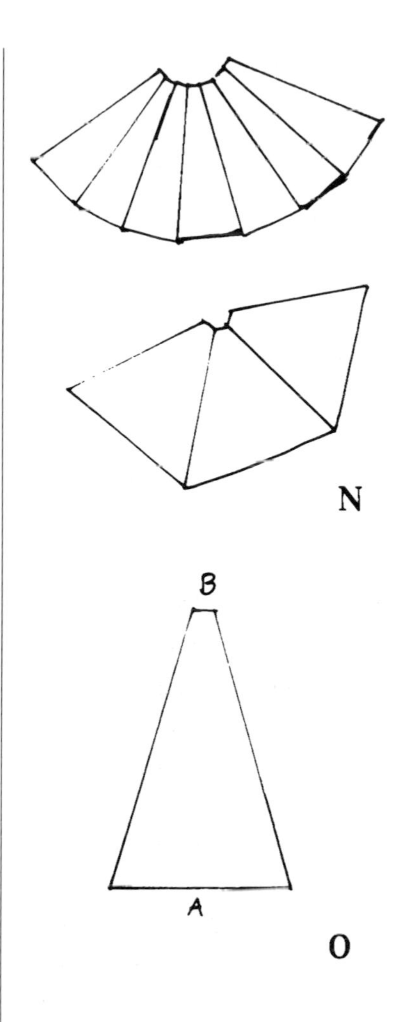

You could also start out with a simple sewing pattern, maybe a pattern that can be sewn in a jersey/knit fabric. Patterns like these are often made without darts or other complicated details. Just remember, a knitted garment has more volume than a sewn one. Full garments, like skirts, become too full when knitted.

To learn more about shaping a garment, take a class in pattern construction and read books on the subject. We have shared philosophy and outlined a few methods in this book. With this you should be able to make some simple designs. Many sewing and knitting magazines show a sketch of a particular garment with its measurements. Use these to practice. Use the measurements from the sketch and figure out the stitch counts using your own swatches.

You can also use patterns made for the yarn you want to knit with or use your own colors and designs in a pattern instead of the given ones. To make your own knitting patterns takes a lot of figuring, but your perserverence will be rewarded with a beautiful, well-fitting garment!

Index

U.S. Suppliers of Rauma Yarns

Charlotte's Web, 137 Epping Road, Exeter, NH 03833. (603) 778-1417. *Mail-order or retail sale of Rauma Finull.*

Nordic Fiber Arts, Four Cutts Road, Durham, NH 03824. (603) 868-1196. *Mail-order or retail sale of Rauma Finull, Istra, and Symfoni.*

Norsk Engros U.S.A., Inc., PO Box 229, Decorah, IA 52101. (800) 553-0014. *Special order wholesale of Rauma Finull, Istra, and Symphoni.*

The Unique, 11 E. Bijou, Colorado Springs, CO 80903. (719) 473-9406. *Mail-order or retail sale of Rauma Finull.*